INTERNATIONAL THEOLOGICAL COMMENTARY

George A. F. Knight and Fredrick Carlson Holmgren
General Editors

GOD'S PEOPLE IN CRISIS

GOD'S PEOPLE IN CRISIS

A Commentary on the Book of

Amos

R. MARTIN-ACHARD

and

A Commentary on the Book of

Lamentations

S. PAUL RE'MI

THE HANDSEL PRESS LTD, EDINBURGH

WM. B. EERDMANS PUBL. CO., GRAND RAPIDS

Copyright © 1984 by The Handsel Press Limited

First published 1984
by William B. Eerdmans Publishing Company
255 Jefferson Avenue, S.E.,
Grand Rapids, MI 49503

and

The Handsel Press Limited
33 Montgomery Street, Edinburgh EH7 5JX

Eerdmans edition 0 8028 1040 3
Handsel edition   0 905312 32 5

CATALOGUING IN PUBLICATION DATA

Martin-Achard, R.
    God's People in Crisis—(International
    Theological Commentary)
    1. Bible. O.T. Lamentations—Commentaries
    2. Bible. O.T. Amos—Commentaries
    I. Title   II. Re'emi, S. Paul   III. Series
    224'.307   BS1535.3

Scripture quotations are from the
Revised Standard Version of the Bible,
Copyrighted 1946, 1952 © 1971, 1973

Printed in Northern Ireland by
The Universities Press (Belfast) Ltd.

CONTENTS

LIST OF ABBREVIATIONS

AV   The Holy Bible, Authorized Version or King James Version (KJV)

LB   The Living Bible

NASB   New American Standard Bible

NEB   The New English Bible

NIV   The Holy Bible, New International Version

RSV   The Holy Bible, Revised Standard Version

SB   La Sainte Bible (The Bible of Jerusalem)

EDITORS' PREFACE

The Old Testament alive in the Church: this is the goal of the *International Theological Commentary*. Arising out of changing, unsettled times, this Scripture speaks with an authentic voice to our own troubled world. It witnesses to God's ongoing purpose and to his caring presence in the universe without ignoring those experiences of life that cause one to question his existence and love. This commentary series is written by front rank scholars who treasure the life of faith.

Addressed to ministers and Christian educators, the *International Theological Commentary* moves beyond the usual critical-historical approach to the Bible and offers a *theological* interpretation of the Hebrew text. The authors of these volumes, therefore, engaging larger textual units of the biblical writings, assist the reader in the appreciation of the theology underlying the text as well as its place in the thought of the Hebrew Scriptures. But more, since the Bible is the book of the believing community, its text in consequence has acquired ever more meaning through an ongoing interpretation. This growth of interpretation may be found both within the Bible itself and in the continuing scholarship of the Church.

Contributors to the *International Theological Commentary* are Christians—persons who affirm the witness of the New Testament concerning Jesus Christ. For Christians, the Bible is *one* scripture containing the Old and New Testaments. For this reason, a commentary on the Old Testament may not ignore the second part of the canon, namely, the New Testament.

Since its beginning, the Church has recognized a special relationship between the two Testaments. But the precise character of this bond has been difficult to define. Thousands of books and articles have discussed the issue. The diversity of views represented in these publications make us aware that the Church is not of one mind in expressing the 'how' of this relationship. The authors of this commentary share a developing consensus that any serious explanation of the Old Testament's relationship to the New will uphold the integrity of the Old Testament. Even though Christianity is rooted in the soil of the Hebrew Scriptures, the biblical interpreter must take care lest he 'christianize' these Scriptures.

Authors writing in this commentary will, no doubt, hold varied views concerning *how* the Old Testament relates to the New. No attempt has been made to dictate one viewpoint in this matter. With the whole Church, we are convinced that the relationship between the two Testaments is real and substantial. But we recognize also the diversity of opinions among Christian scholars when they attempt to articulate fully the nature of this relationship.

In addition to the Christian Church, there exists another people for whom the Old Testament is important, namely, the Jewish community. Both Jews and Christians claim the Hebrew Bible as Scripture. Jews believe that the basic teaching of this Scripture point toward, and are developed by, the Talmud, which assumed its present form about A.D. 500. Christians, on the other hand, hold that the Old Testament finds its fulfilment in the New Testament. The Hebrew Bible, therefore, 'belongs' to both the Church and the Synagogue.

Recent studies have demonstrated how profoundly early Christianity reflects a Jewish character. This fact is not surprising because the Christian movement arose out of the context of first-century Judaism. Further, Jesus himself was Jewish, as were the first Christians. It is to be expected, therefore, that Jewish and Christian interpretations of the Hebrew Bible will reveal similarities *and* disparities. Such is the case. The authors of the *International Theological Commentary* will refer to the various Jewish traditions that they consider important for an appreciation of the Old Testament text. Such references will enrich our understanding of certain biblical passages and, as an extra gift, offer us insight into the relationship of Judaism to early Christianity.

An important second aspect of the present series is its *international* character. In the past, Western church leaders were considered to be *the* leaders of the Church—at least by those living in the West! The theology and biblical exegesis done by these scholars dominated the thinking of the Church. Most commentaries were produced in the Western world and reflected the lifestyle, needs, and thoughts of its civilization. But the Christian Church is a worldwide community. People who belong to this universal Church reflect differing thoughts, needs, and lifestyles.

Today the fastest growing churches in the world are to be found not in the West, but in Africa, Indonesia, South America, Korea, Taiwan, and elsewhere. By the end of this century, Christians in these areas will outnumber those who live in the West. In our age, especially, a commentary on the Bible must transcend the parochialism of Western civilization and be sensitive to issues that are the special problems of persons who live outside of the 'Christian' West, issues such as race relations, personal survival and fulfilment, liberation, revolution, famine, tyranny, disease, war, the poor, religion and state. Inspired of God, the authors of the Old Testament knew what life is like on the edge of existence. They addressed themselves to everyday people who often faced more than everyday problems. Refusing to limit God to the 'spiritual,' they portrayed him as one who heard and knew the cries of people in pain (see Exod. 3:7–8). The contributors to the *International Theological Commentary* are persons who prize the writings of these biblical authors as a word of life to our world today. They read the Hebrew Scriptures in the twin contexts of ancient Israel and our modern day.

The scholars selected as contributors underscore the international aspect of the Commentary. Representing very different geographical, ideological, and ecclesiastical backgrounds, they come from over seventeen countries. Besides scholars from such traditional countries as England, Scotland, France, Italy, Switzerland, Canada, New Zealand, Australia, South Africa, and the United States, contributors from the following places are included: Israel, Indonesia, India, Thailand, Singapore, Taiwan, and countries of Eastern Europe. Such diversity makes for richness of thought. Christian scholars living in Buddhist, Muslim, or Socialist lands may be able to offer the World Church insights into the biblical message—insights to which the scholarship of the West could be blind.

The proclamation of the biblical message is the focal concern of the *International Theological Commentary*. Generally speaking, the authors of these commentaries value the historical-critical studies of past scholars, but they are convinced that these studies by themselves are not enough. The Bible is more than an object of critical study; it is the revelation of God. In the written Word, God has disclosed himself and his will to humankind. Our authors see themselves as servants of the Word which, when rightly received, brings *shalom* to both the individual and the community.

—GEORGE A. F. KNIGHT
—FREDRICK CARLSON HOLMGREN

THE END OF THE PEOPLE OF GOD

A Commentary on the Book of

Amos

R. MARTIN-ACHARD

translated by G. A. F. Knight

CONTENTS

INTRODUCTION

Amos is the earliest of the prophets of Israel whose words have been preserved for us. He appears during the long and apparently glorious reign of Jeroboam II (around 786–746 B.C.), before the people of Yahweh had to undergo their terrible confrontation with Assyria. His name derives from the root *amas* which means to lift up, carry, take away, and it is probably a diminutive of Amaziah (2 Chron. 17:16). It seems to express recognition of, or the requesting of divine aid: 'Yahweh has carried, taken away (a load), and so has delivered'; (or, 'Yahweh delivers, rescues', cf. Ps. 68:20; Isa. 46:3). Note that we must not confuse the prophet *Amos* with Isaiah's father, *Amots*, as is sometimes done.

Amos belonged originally to the south, to the township of Tekoa in Judah (1:1; 7:12). It was situated some 9 km from Bethlehem and 18 from Jerusalem, in a rather hilly region bordering on the desert of Judah. This region lent itself to the rearing of smaller livestock like goats and sheep rather than to agriculture. It was not desert, as is often said, nor was Tekoa a miserable little village lost in a barren countryside; rather, ever since David's day it seems to have been an important centre (cf. 2 Sam. 14:2). According to 2 Chron. 11:5 f, Rehoboam had fortified it to secure the defence of the south. So Amos had the opportunity to live in a place whose political, cultural and agrarian role was by no means negligible. Thus his attitude with regard to the big northern cities, such as Samaria and Bethel, does not express primarily the hostility of a countryman towards a civilization that he discovers to be altogether one of luxury and corruption.

Meanwhile Amos spends his time with the beasts for which he is responsible. He knows nature well. He observes the *'shooting up of the latter growth'* (7:1); he marks the arrival of the locusts (4:9) and the roaring of a lion (3:4); he knows what a drought means for the flocks as well as for man (4:7 f; 8:11 f); he notices ripe summer fruits (8:1), the bird caught in a snare (3:5), the snake hidden in a hole in the wall of a house (5:19). This is because he lives amongst the shepherds of Tekoa (1:1). The term *noqed* that occurs here

3

probably means a special category of sheep breeder (cf. 2 Kgs. 3:4). A *noqed* is not, as has been maintained at times, a functionary attached to a sanctuary charged with foretelling the future. Thus Amos would not be just a simple shepherd, but the manager, perhaps even the owner, of a small flock.

At his meeting with the high priest of Bethel he calls himself a 'herdsman', or better, one who is responsible for a flock, from which task Yahweh 'took me' to go and witness to his will before the northern kingdom (7:14). He adds that he is also a *'dresser of sycamore trees'*, whose fruits, once they are cut open, become sweet enough to be used as food for domestic animals and even for those who tend them. The Hebrew term *boles*, used here, might bear the sense of mixing, blending, pointing to Amos' occupation as he mixed the foodstuffs his flock required.

What indications we can put together from the book of Amos (1:1; 7:14) lead us to understand that the prophet was no mere impoverished employee, reduced more or less to penury; he was a man socially and economically independent. He seems even to have been a man of means, or at least to have held a position of some importance. Because of this his handling of the situation with regard to Samaria and its élite does not depend on the class struggle but on the vocation that his God has laid upon him.

This southerner is brusquely snatched from his natural element and surroundings, as was Abraham (Gen. 12:1 ff), David (1 Sam. 16 ff), Peter (Luke 5) and Paul (Acts 9), in order to intervene in the northern kingdom, where material conditions were quite different. His mission fell between the years 760 and 750 B.C., probably nearer the earlier of these dates. In general, we have to realize that Amos appeared in the kingdom of Jeroboam II in a period of great ostentation. No one of course imagined that they were living in a period immediately preceding a military and political disaster marked by the appearance on the scene of the great Assyrian conqueror Tiglath Pileser III, around 745 B.C. Actually Amos never mentions this sovereign, and never specifically names Assyria as Yahweh's bearer of judgment, just the contrary of Isaiah (Isa. 10:5 ff). The latter called him God's executor of justice. Amos seems to have dealt with a population with no anxieties about its future. It was preoccupied with dreams of grandeur and a thirst for pleasure (5:10 ff; 6:1 ff).

Amos must have visited in the north for a period of some months, probably slightly over a year. He must have gone to the capital city, Samaria. However, it is at Bethel that he reveals himself, the spiritual centre of the State (7:10 ff). He must have been expelled the day after his encounter with Amaziah, for no

4

mention is made of him thereafter. It is probable that he then returned to the south and resumed his former activities. It is moving to think that his mission, which lasted such a short time, had in the end such reverberations that his ancient words have remained vividly alive throughout twenty-eight centuries right till our time. One would like to know what happened to him when he returned to live in Judah. But that, like his calling, belongs to the secret of God. (A Jewish legend suggests that he met a brutal end, in that he was struck to death by Amaziah's son!) Like the majority of Yahweh's witnesses, but in a manner even more vivid than most, he was called to be the bearer of the Word to Israel. He fulfilled his function—and then he disappeared; and yet, 'he is still speaking' (Heb. 11:4).

Whatever then was the end of the prophet? It is probable that, having returned to Judah, he made a profoundly important decision. He decided to set down in writing the utterances that God had charged him to proclaim in Israel, and to entrust them to one or other of his disciples (Isa. 8:16 ff; Jer. 36). It is owing to this initiative that we, even today, can hear through the words of Amos translated into our modern languages the divine Word. His words catch up with us now in our time and challenge us in our concrete situations.

His Book

The book of Amos is actually a collection of his utterances or oracles, including some autobiographical elements (the 'visions' of chap. 7 ff), as well as the passage describing the confrontation between Amos and Amaziah (7:10–17). One can divide this collection of nine chapters into three main sections: (1) 1:3–2:16, oracles against the nations neighbouring on the northern kingdom and against Israel itself; (2) 3:1–6:14, a series of pronouncements against Israel, and in particular against its 'élite', real or supposed, (3) 7:1–9:10, visions accompanied by statements announcing the end of the State of Israel. These collections are preceded by an introduction (for the title and prefatory material, see 1:1 f), and there is a conclusion (9:11–15) whose positive tone contrasts with what precedes it.

We should remember that the prophets of Israel were not writers in the first place, but men of the Word (Jer. 18:18). It was only necessity that impelled them to set down their words in writing. When they were not listened to by their contemporaries they had necessarily to formulate their witness to some degree in a written form if it was to serve as witness to the Truth whose willing servants they were.

Amos' utterances were, then, first of all spoken; they were intended to be heard with all their intonations, their plays on words, their rhythms, their associations of sounds and images. All this oratorical art was employed by the prophet to make himself into Yahweh's spokesman in face of the people of Samaria and Bethel. Our best translations, even when rendered as faithfully as possible, reproduce his utterances only imperfectly. We need take only one example. One day Amos sees a basket of ripe fruit, fruits ripened at the end of summer, *qaits*. He discovers at the same moment that Yahweh is announcing the end, *qets*, of Israel. The time is ripe for the judgment of a people that is clearly intractable before its God (8:1–2).

As much as possible, then, we in our turn should *speak* these prophetic utterances; we should not be content with just reading them with our eyes. We should proclaim them, using our voice, our breath, our whole body, so that they imprint themselves upon us and become our very flesh!

Like almost every book of the Bible, the book of Amos has had a *history*. It was not composed at one sitting. The first collection of '*the words of Amos*' (1:1) goes back to the prophet himself, along with various groupings of material like those of the oracles against foreign peoples (1:3 ff). There we hear declarations about the iniquity that prevails in the northern kingdom (around chapter 5), or again about the cycle of his 'visions' (chapter 7 ff). This collection has been carefully preserved by his disciples, close to or distant from the shepherd of Tekoa, since events alas, proved him right. The catastrophe that he had announced to a blind and insensitive generation surpassed what anyone could have imagined. Samaria was taken by the Assyrians in 721, its population massacred or deported, and the northern kingdom wiped completely off the map.

The book of Amos also contains notes, glosses and annotations, all made by his Judean readers. These date from the period that followed Amos' intrusion, perhaps as early as the time of Josiah (between 622 and 609 B.C.), or else later on after the southern kingdom had disappeared. That was in 587 B.C., when in its turn Jerusalem fell beneath the blows of the successors and heirs of the Assyrians: the Babylonians. Perhaps people then felt the need to link the message of Amos with that of Judah, or to set a limit to a message that was above all negative by including a word of consolation. This pointed to the fact that beyond the judgment on the people of Yahweh to which Amos had made himself witness, the God of Israel remained free to rebuild what had been destroyed, and to give life to what, humanly speaking, seemed to be completely dead (cf. for example, Ezek. 36 f).

The book of Amos then, like other biblical writings, reveals within it traces of rewriting. (This fact witnesses to the importance for future generations of the faithful preservation of these writings.) The annotations, the qualifications, the setting in order that they contain participate in the revelation of Yahweh to his people, and through them to us. But to understand Amos' intrusion twenty-eight centuries ago it is important for us to distinguish between what goes back directly to him and what is the work of his successors. Certain passages are particularly subject to discussion. According to some exegetes, but not all, they clearly represent late alterations. Such in particular are 1:2, which could well be from the hand of a Judean disciple of the prophet; and 4:13; 5:8 f; 9:5 f, which seem to recall a hymn in honour of Yahweh. These passages were thus probably introduced into the text later on. Then there are the declarations on Tyre (1:9 f), on Edom (1:11 f), and particularly on Judah (2:4 ff). All these would be secondary. Finally, the conclusion of the collection (9:11 ff; or 9:13, or again 9:8 ff) would be the finishing touch of an editor living after the fall of the house of David (9:11), that is to say, after 587, for it adds a note of consolation to those Judeans who had survived the disaster.

These remarks are not meant to detract from the value of the notes and redactional glosses in the book of Amos; rather they are meant to recognize the fact that the message of the prophet has accompanied the history of his people and continues to nourish the faith of the faithful by the warnings, and indictments, the judgments and the words of hope that they never cease to find there. The book of Amos thus participates in the living tradition of the people of God.

His Message

The prophet's appearance within the kingdom of Jeroboam II is characterized by its harshness, by the severity of the diagnosis that Amos makes of the state of the people of Israel, and by the rigorous judgment which Yahweh pronounces upon the guilty. Taken as a whole, as well as in its various sections, the book of Amos concentrates on the announcement of *the end* of the northern State and at the same time justifies this radical condemnation. Night falls on the people of Yahweh; the menace is there, ever so near, of a disaster without precedent. An atmosphere of panic seizes the cities and the countryside. The images that the prophet keeps constantly returning to are those of *flight*, *ruin*, and *death*.

7

The great oracle against the nations reaches its climax in an apocalyptic vision of an army in confusion, the soldiers routed, seeking in vain for safety in flight (2:13 ff), the winter houses and the summer houses that were the pride of their owners, suddenly collapsing, stricken by some mysterious cataclysm (3:13 f). Further on, the prophet intones a song of lamentation over the house of Israel (5:1 f), which has fallen to rise no more. Here, in all the public squares, the hour is one of lamenting and of cries of anguish (5:16 f); there, in the ruins of people's homes, dead bodies are being burnt in ghastly silence (6:8 ff). Amos proclaims precisely: 'This is no longer the time for pardon; the respite of grace is ended; the hour of the end has come' (7:7 ff; 8:1 f). He then depicts the destruction of the sanctuary (9:1 f), specifying that no one will survive the divine wrath (9:1 ff). Death is everywhere; she climbs up the walls of the cities, she penetrates into people's homes, she takes possession of the streets, she reaches out to the open country... such is the verdict that Yahweh has pronounced against his own.

Despite some appeals to return to Yahweh (5:4 f, 14 f), and various allusions to those who will be 'the remnant of Joseph' after the disaster (3:12; 5:2, 15), Amos appears quite clearly as the witness of a God who pronounces a radical *No* to the very existence, both present and future, of his people. Moreover, this No should be heard by us too just as much as it should have been listened to by the prophet's contemporaries. Here was a people resting on their past, and particularly on the kindnesses that Yahweh had showered upon them. Yet they could only dream of profiting from the benefits they had received and of reaping advantage from them. So the prophets, and Amos was the first to do so, had the formidable mission of announcing that the history of relations between God and his people ('salvation history'?) was now finished; it had no more significance, nor could it offer any security any more. All they could reckon on from that moment was what Yahweh was preparing for, or rather, *against* Israel. It was as if the ground had suddenly been snatched from under the feet of the Israelites—the picture of an earthquake often appears in Amos—who found themselves all at once at the mercy of the wrath of Yahweh even while they were living comfortably in the fantasy that they were 'the chosen people' (3:1 f).

Amos is not satisfied with merely proclaiming the judgment that God is pronouncing against the northern kingdom. He goes on to justify it by an indictment that unmasks the hypocrisy of its inhabitants, the venality of its judges (5:10 f), the appetite that Samaria's privileged classes has for the pursuit of pleasure (4:1 f;

8

6:1 ff), the extent of social oppression in Israel that brought about the humiliation of the needy, the trampling down of the poor, the cheating of the hapless (2:6 ff; 8:4 ff). For a mere nothing, on the ground that 'business is business', for just a pair of sandals, see how they go about selling a man who has no resources (2:6; 8:6). The book of Amos is thus one long accusation against the Israelites, against the greed of the merchants, the indifference of the authorities (4 f; 6:1 ff; 8:4 ff), the hypocrisy of the public prayers. In short, the northern kingdom is condemned for having repeatedly violated justice in contempt for the rights of the most deprived; and so it has witnessed to the contempt in which it actually holds God himself.

Such is Amos' message, recalled briefly in these few lines. We have to accept it in all its severity; its intransigence takes into account the uncompromising character of the God of Israel when it is a question of the dignity of 'the least of these my brethren' (Matt. 25:40). There is no question of correcting the prophet's words to make them more bearable. We must just accept Amos for what he is, one witness amongst others whose message, in all of its inflexibility, must be listened to and retained. The Gospel does not in fact make us take his indictment and his verdict, pronounced twenty-eight centuries ago, any less seriously; on the contrary, it should show us its truth and its relevance for today.

His Influence

In his condemnation of Israelite society Amos agrees with most of the prophets who are part and parcel of the people of Yahweh and whose message has been preserved for us. In turn, Isaiah (Isa. 1:10 ff; 5:1 ff), Hosea (Hos. 4:1 ff; 6:4 ff), Micah (Mic. 3:1 ff; 6:1 ff), Jeremiah (Jer. 7:1 ff), and those who came after them, all denounced the abuses committed by Jerusalem and Samaria—the hypocrisy of a cult which the 'haves' used as an alibi, the meantime showing no consideration for the weakest members of the community. They then announced the pitiless measures that Yahweh was going to take against the guilty. From Amos to Malachi, each of the spokesmen of Israel's God, in his own words and in his own particular style, thus assured his hearers that the lengthy lawsuit that God had conducted against his own ones would be continued, relayed to each in turn, for the honour of his Name and for the salvation of the 'poor'.

Amos is probably one of the most severe in his condemnation of Israel. But, curiously enough, that aspect of his message seems to have been scarcely noticed by posterity. That which constitutes the uniqueness of his appearance in history, his criticism of the social conditions amongst the people of Yahweh, has remained marginal both in the Jewish and in the Christian traditions. The New Testament cites only two of Amos' pronouncements. The one (5:25–27, to be found quoted in Acts 7:42 f), allows the author of Acts to underline the guilt (that is to say, the idolatry) of the people of Moses. The other (9:11 f), made use of in Acts 15:13 ff, but quoted from the LXX (the Greek Version of the Old Testament), provides the Jerusalem council with the opportunity to resolve the thorny question of the status of Christians of pagan origin. We should note that these two texts are used in the same way in the literature of Qumran.

The Church was to see in Amos, before all else, a witness to Christ and the Church. So it is in the case of Saint Augustine, who cites Amos 9:11 f in his 'The City of God' (18:28). With the exception of the Reformer of Florence, Savonarola, who was to preach in the Lenten season of 1496 on the books of Amos and Zechariah—two years before he was executed—and whose language was to recall the vigorous and threatening style of the prophet of the 8th century B.C., it would be almost necessary to await our 20th century for his social message to be heard again and to be brought to mind, notably in certain Christian and Socialist circles. But these have been more or less on the margin of the ecclesiastical and political 'Establishment'. We should note, for example, that the Jewish, Marxist philospher Ernst Bloch, in Germany, attached great importance to the preaching of the shepherd of Tekoa on justice; for Amos bore witness to the idea of 'dis-alienation' in face of an oppressive society that had traditionally leaned on the official Church.

This 'atheistic' reading of Amos is indicative of a secularized world, as western civilization is, in that it pays no attention to the fundamental purpose of the prophet. For he sought to confront his contemporaries with the true God, the God of Israel, and not with what their appetite for influence and their thirst for pleasure had created. Amos presents himself at Bethel, as at Samaria, as Yahweh's witness. It is to him that he owed his mission; it is he who imposes on Amos a message whose gravity does not escape the prophet. It is his voice that we have to listen to in our turn through his twenty-eight centuries old words. Amos thus sends us back to his God, who is simultaneously the God of Abraham, Isaac and Jacob, and so also the God of Jesus Christ.

Part I

COMMENTARY

Amos 1:1–2

Like most of the prophetical books, the book of Amos begins with *an historical note* (cf. Isa. 1:1; Jer. 1:1; Mic. 1:1) that has a double purpose. It introduces him as Yahweh's spokesman, and it places his appearance at a point of time. The text here has been particularly worked over, doubtless as the result of various editorial modifications. The initial title might well have been: 'The words of Amos of Tekoa (against Israel two years before the earthquake)', with the mention of the reigns of Uzziah of Judah and of Jeroboam II of Israel being the most recently added element. We should note the direct bond established here as elsewhere in the O.T. between the Word and the Vision, or alternatively between the Seer and the Prophet (Isa. 1:1; Obad. 1; Mic. 1:1; and especially 1 Sam. 9:9). For it is a question in either case of the revelation that Yahweh is transmitting to his witness so that he can pass it on to his people. The prophet is not necessarily a visionary. What happens is that Yahweh speaks to him by scenes at which he is present or by means of objects that he contemplates (cf. Amos 7 ff; Jer. 1), while, in a complementary manner, the divine Word permits this herald of the God of Israel to 'see' what had to date escaped his contemporaries; in other words, to read off the reality in the way God understands it and not as his brethren, even the wisest amongst them. One often gets the impression that the prophets are ahead of their time. They already discern what will be manifested tomorrow to the eyes of all but which today remains veiled from the sight of the majority of the people, and particularly from those in positions of responsibility.

This first verse of Amos also informs us that the prophet, whoever he may be, is *tied to a particular time*, and that his message is meant for *a particular moment* in the destiny of the people of God. The prophetic message presupposes a particular historical and geographical framework, as well as that of a precise economic and cultural situation. It is just this that at times renders the reading of

Amos difficult for us, for he is addressing a specific people in circumstances that he knows well. He turns up at Bethel and at Samaria in the time of king Jeroboam II; and in spite of the progress we have made in our knowledge of Israel's past, thanks notably to archaeological research, many of the elements in the history of the 8th century in the Syro-Palestinian region still elude us.

The God of the Scriptures does not act in a vague, impersonal manner. His interventions are seen to be with real and factual people and in particular places and times. His Word is not fulfilled in generalities or in mere principles. It is the same today as it was yesterday. Thus it is that when we study as carefully as possible what happened in former times or what was said in bygone days *at other times and in other places*, the divine Word meets up with us *in our own situations* and its *relevance* suddenly becomes apparent to us. Setting oneself to listen to Amos is ultimately to discover how greatly the prophet helps us to read our own time and to see our own century as Yahweh sees it.

The note at v. 1 speaks of two kings, the one in Judah and the other in Israel, for the empire founded by David had split into two States following upon the reign of Solomon. We should note that geography plays a central role in the destiny of Yahweh's people, though it is often neglected by readers of the O.T. Israel found herself situated, in fact, in an area that lacked any cohesion, whether geographically, climatically, economically or culturally speaking. She had to live in a land made up of separate sections. More particularly that land lay at the extreme limit of the Asiatic continent, not far from Africa and not much more from Europe. So it was condemned to suffer from the two-way political pressures of the great powers of the region. These pushed first east then west, then north then south, as they sought to control the Syro-Palestinian region. Thus Israel could scarcely hope to conduct an autonomous policy. This was because, for one reason or another, Egypt on the one hand and the Assyrians and the Babylonians on the other were not in a position to play a part in an area of the world that never ceased to be coveted. That is precisely what happened about the year 1000 B.C. in the time of David, and a little later in the first half of the 8th century under the regions of Uzziah of Judah and of Jeroboam II of Israel. Jeroboam II profited also from the temporary overthrow of a formidable enemy, the kingdom of Syria that lay to the north and was peopled by Arameans. Following his father Joash, the Israelite king was thus able to reconquer Transjordan (2 Kgs. 13:25; 2 Kgs. 14:25, 28 (?); cf. also Amos 6:14). The frontiers of the state of Israel to the north then almost coincided with those of the ancient Davidic empire. But the Assyrians, tied up for a time in annexing the Syro-Palestinian region politically, were able to impose their might upon the group of little States of that area, once Tiglath-Pileser III had succeeded to the throne of Assyria.

Historians in general hold that the reigns of Uzziah (Azariah—about 783–742) and of Jeroboam II (about 786–746) were prosperous for both Judah and Israel. Moreover, both kings were successful at the expense of either their Edomite neighbours (2 Kgs. 14:22) or the Arameans (2 Kgs. 13:25; 14:25). All this led people to believe that the '*Day of the Lord*' (Amos 5:18 ff) would mark the apotheosis, the climax, of an activity that up till now had been crowned with success.

The economic situation profited from these favourable circumstances, the ruling class in the cities benefiting particularly. International trade developed, and houses were improved along with their furnishings (3:10; 5:11; 3:12; 6:4). But division developed right at the heart of Yahweh's people, in so far as a minority, grouped round the court and settled in the capital city, increased its power and its resources, while the mass of the people, notably in the country, saw themselves dispossessed of their means and condemned to lead a pitiful existence. The coming of Amos fitted into this context of inequality, which could not be hidden by the grandiose nature of the festivals in honour of the national God (5:21 ff). Israel was going to pay very dearly for the ephemeral glory that they were then experiencing under Jeroboam II. Some thirty years later Israel had ceased to exist as an independent State, while its elite was to disappear for ever in the deportation!

v. 2   *The Introduction*

This verse, which begins the 'Amos collection', in a sense sums up the essentials of his message. Some exegetes attribute it to a disciple of the prophet who lived in Jerusalem and who was concerned to place at the head of the words of his master a solemn declaration, drawing his inspiration from some liturgical formula. Yet this verse consists less of an oracle than of a hymn, one that exalts the God who had made Zion his city ever since David had installed there 'the Ark of the Covenant'. This had been the sign and seal of God's presence in Israel's midst (2 Sam. 6; Ps. 132). The verse is carefully constructed; verse 2a announces the divine intervention, and verse 2b shows the consequences thereof.

One receives here a picture, familiar to Amos as a keeper of livestock, of a lion roaring (3:4, 8) and causing terror, and before which there is nothing to do but flee (5:19). This motif is to be found also in other prophets (Hos. 5:14; Isa. 5:29; etc.), even on into the N.T. (1 Pet. 5:8). The lion's roar in this verse is used in parallel with 'the voice of Yahweh', recalling those mighty and terrifying manifestations in the course of which the God of Israel revealed himself to his people (cf. Exod. 19). The Psalms sing traditionally of 'Yahweh who gives forth his voice', or, in other words, 'who thunders forth' in the course of an electric storm, as in Pss. 18:14; 68:34, and especially in 29:3 ff. It is a question of the classical demonstration of the power of the divine, or better still, of the holiness of Yahweh, before which nothing at all can stand (Jud. 5:4 f; Deut. 32:22; Hab. 3:3 ff; etc.). In v. 2a then, there is mixed in with Amos's own experience a tradition that goes back into the far past of Israel so that we are placed in the presence of the sovereign, active, terrible God, whose Word, transmitted by the shepherd of Tekoa, is addressed directly to the inhabitants of the northern kingdom.

Verse 2b discloses the sad consequences for the country and for its inhabitants of Yahweh's intervention. The pastures where the shepherds, amongst whom Amos is included (1:1; 7:14), were accustomed to lead their flocks, *mourn* for their vegetation *withers* as in the dry season when the whole of nature seems to be stricken to death. We should note that the author can make play with the double meaning of the Hebrew word *abelu*. It comes from the root *abal* which means both to be in mourning and to be dried up. Carmel, which was known for its flourishing vegetation, would become a miserable and sterile area, destined for death, with its glory turned into confusion. This is suggested by the verb *yabesh*, to become parched, which evokes by assonance with the verb *bosh* ideas of shame and dishonour.

Briefly, then, according to verses 1 and 2, Yahweh is about to reveal himself in his formidable grandeur, which will result only in ruin and misery for his people. The book of Amos begins therefore with a threat of death that hovers over the kingdom of Jeroboam II, and on which Amos' oracles will comment at length and which they will confirm.

Finally, we should note that the hymnic element in Amos 1:2 recurs, in different contexts, in Joel 3:16 and in a late passage in the book of Jeremiah (Jer. 25:30).

ORACLES AGAINST FOREIGN NATIONS AND AGAINST ISRAEL
(AMOS 1:3–2:16)

This fine long poem is composed of a series of declarations by the prophet in the name of the God of Israel. These are not directed at humanity in general, nor even at the great powers of the east (Mesopotamia) or of the south (Egypt); they are directed at the immediate neighbours of the people of Yahweh.

From a first reading of these chapters it would appear that the prophet's oracles all seem to be constructed alike with the exception of the last one (2:6–16), which is particularly developed either intentionally, or because it was completed after the others.

Each of Amos' utterances comprises four elements:

(1) An introductory formula, in classical prophetic language, which recalls the style used by a messenger: '*Thus says the Lord . . .*'

(2) A general declaration that is virtually identical in each case, meant to point to the culpability of the nation as seen in its relationship to Yahweh, and so bring about the judgment to follow: '*For three transgressions of . . . and for four, I will not revoke . . .*'. We should note that here Amos uses the term *pesha'*, the word indicating that the peoples in question are in a state of rebellion vis-à-vis the God of Israel. The expression: '*For three . . . and for four*' reminds us of the Wisdom literature (Prov. 6:16 ff; 30:15 f). It implies a multiplicity of faults, only one of which however is mentioned explicitly by the prophet. The words '*I will not revoke* . . . (RSV; we should note that the word 'punishment' to be found in the KJV does not occur in the Hebrew) are translated in various ways. They are equivalent to 'I will not revoke my judgment', underlining the fact that the decision taken by Yahweh against the guilty is final.

(3) There then follows the verdict pronounced by Yahweh, who intervenes personally against Damascus, Gaza, Tyre, etc. (Notice the divine 'I' at vv. 4, 5, 7, 8, etc.). The punishment consists usually of the sending of fire (vv. 4, 7, 10, 12, etc.). This motif may have been borrowed from the theme of the holy war.

(4) Certain strophes (vv. 5, 8, 15, etc.) contain again a concluding formula, '*says the Lord Yahweh*', recalling forcibly that the prophetic word is but an echo of the divine judgment.

What the prophet says on the subject of the kingdom of Samaria (2:5–16) is developed in more detail. We note that the act of accusation here extends to various crimes for which Israel can be censured (vv. 6b–8). On the other hand, the text adds an historical reminiscence that mentions all that Yahweh has done for his people (vv. 9–12). The last verses (vv. 13–16) announce the judgment on the guilty under the shape of a catastrophe, either a military one or a natural event, from which even the bravest will not escape. It is on this assertion that Amos' inaugural poem ends.

These chapters contain a number of references of a geographical and historical nature. Some of these are hard to pinpoint, yet we will not dwell on them for lack of space. We might refer the reader to the various histories of Israel or to the works that deal with biblical geography. But the collection of proper names that we find here reminds us once more that the God of the Bible concerns himself not with some imaginary world but with our earth, and with the history of the nations to be found on it. It is also striking to see with what precision Amos evokes both past and contemporary events. These involve the fate of the nations of the Syro-Palestinian region vis-à-vis their God. He witnesses by this means to the continuing interest that Israel's God expresses for people in circumstances that are particularly their own.

We might examine each word that Amos addresses to one or another of the peoples in 1:3–2:16, each being a case on its own, and note how effectively the prophet deals in succession with a whole series of guilty nations. But Amos' statements here are not simply juxtaposed one next to the other as is the case in other chapters dealing with the pagan nations; they are linked by the prophet himself to form a unity. He underlines this by the way he uses identical formulas throughout this whole passage.

Amos' intention, perhaps inspired by a like Egyptian model (it can be compared with the words of these 'execration texts' that date from the beginning of the second millenium; but this point remains open to discussion) is to denounce the guilt of the nations who are neighbours to Yahweh's people, to the north and to the south, to the east and to the west; but the prophet does not stop there. To the surprise of all he attacks the kingdom of Israel itself and lingers at length over its faults and its condemnation. The last strophe (2:6–16) seems to be the culmination of the prophetic discourse; throughout his list of charges against Damascus, Gaza and Moab he is thinking also, and already, of Samaria.

One can picture the prophet finding himself one day in the capital city. He mixes with the crowd on a market and festival day. There he finds Israelites coming from the countryside, foreign merchants hurrying in from all over, and the presence of civil and religious authorities. Suddenly a voice makes itself heard, someone is denouncing Aram (Syria), the old enemy who has made Israel suffer a-plenty. People listen, nonplussed; they approve, they applaud. Then comes Gaza's turn to be arraigned and there come to mind those interminable confrontations with the Philistines that Israel had endured ever since she had occupied the land. This unknown character now continues with his diatribe whilst the crowd experiences a thrill of light-hearted nationalism. Then all at once the mysterious orator is speaking about Israel herself, using the threatening tone he had employed till now for the other

nations. Now he is denouncing first one and then another of
Samaria's crimes. To finish with, he calls to mind, before the
scandalized crowd, a scene of panic. It is highly possible that a
scene such as this was the basis of the text that we read today at
the beginning of the book of Amos!

(a) Against Damascus (1:3–5)

This strophe is constructed in the classical manner: Amos speaks in
the name of Yahweh (v. 3a); he denounces first in a general
manner (v. 3b) and then in particular (v. 3c) the crimes of
Damascus and announces the punishment of the Arameans
(Syrians) (v. 4 f). If the list of crimes is brief but explicit, the
prophet lays stress on the verdict, which he has said is of an
irrevocable nature. The region of Gilead was the cause that the
Israelites and the Arameans disputed so bitterly, notably under
Ben-hadad (1 Kgs. 15:18 ff), under Ben-hadad II (1 Kgs. 20:22),
under the usurper Ben-hadad III (2 Kgs. 13:3, 7). Note that the
name Hadad appears in that of the god Hadad, the god of the
storm, and the equivalent of the god whom the Old Testament
calls the Canaanite Baal.

Amos aims here probably at the last of the kings whose
interference in Transjordan took place before the defeat of the
Arameans by Assyria, or possibly even in the 9th century. The
prophet does not reproach Damascus because of its struggle for the
occupation of Gilead, but for the treatment that it inflicted on the
vanquished. This revealed a desire to wipe out an unfortunate
population—*'They have threshed Gilead with threshing sledges of iron'*, an
expression perhaps to be taken literally, or else at least
symbolically (2 Sam. 12:31; Isa. 41:15). In any case it reveals the
frightful cruelty of which the Arameans were guilty.

Yahweh's response is in proportion to the crimes Syria has
committed. The royal palaces are to be committed to the flames (v.
4), Damascus forced to capitulate (this was to take place in reality
in 732 when the city was captured by Tiglath-Pileser III), the
inhabitants of the area exterminated (v. 5b), and above all Syria
was to go into exile to their place of origin. According to Amos 9:7
this was *qir* (v. 5b). It was as if the Arameans were to be effaced
from history. They were to be the victims of total war for having
shown no pity upon their vanquished foes. Yahweh is here acting
as Judge on behalf of a population that is defenceless before the
occupying power.

(b) Against the Philistine Cities (1:6–8)

Yahweh turns here to the cities founded by the Philistines and in first place to Gaza, the most important amongst them (vv. 6 f). The sanctions pronounced against these guilty cities by the prophet are practically the same as those against Damascus—strongholds destroyed, their inhabitants massacred, dynasties overthrown, the Philistines' whole political and military system abolished (vv. 7 f). We should note once again that the God of Israel takes the initiative in this judicial action.

Yahweh does not reproach the Philistines so much for their raids against their neighbours—in fact the Israelites are not singled out or named; their crime is the enslaving of their captives (cf. 1 Sam. 30:1 f) and organizing on a grand scale a veritable traffic in 'displaced persons', in order to hand them over to the Edomites who would then sell them again further south (v. 6c).

(c) Against Tyre (1:9–10)

This oracle, shorter than those preceding it, is lacking in originality. So it might be dated to a period later than that of Amos. Once again the guilty party is accused of carrying on a traffic to the detriment of human beings whose identity is not determined precisely; but the context suggests that it has to do with members of the people of Yahweh.

What is most remarkable in this strophe is the reference to a 'covenant of brotherhood' (v. 9c). This is probably a reference to the traditional friendly relations that obtained between Israel and Tyre (1 Kgs. 5:1; 9:13; 16:30 ff). Yahweh reproaches Tyre with having been unfaithful to its pledged word and with having destroyed a time-honoured trust when it also delivered for sale 'a whole people' (v. 9c) to Syria, a near neighbour of Phoenicia. This reading is more probable than 'Edom'. It needs the change of only one letter in Hebrew.

(d) Against Edom (1:11–12)

This strophe is often attributed to a later period (6th century?), since it seems to be an echo of the political situation of the Edomites at the moment when the kingdom of Judah succumbed to the infinitely superior forces of the Babylonians. Instead of coming to the help of a people to whom they were bound by a degree of parental unity (Gen. 25:15 ff) Edom was delighted at its destruction (Obad. 10 ff), and had sung when Jerusalem was in extremities: 'Rase it, rase it! Down to the foundations!' (Ps. 137:7; cf. also Ezek. 25:12–14; 35:1 ff). The author of v. 10 conjures up the fury with which Edom had persecuted the people of Yahweh. To this longstanding hatred the answer was to be that of fire: Teman was to be burned, the strongholds of Bozrah were to go up in flames (v. 12). Here is a picture of war waged without pity but which a pitiless nation had brough upon itself—'All who take the sword will perish by the sword'! (Matt. 26:52).

(e) Against Ammon (1:13–15)

In this announcement in the classical form, Yahweh reproaches a people who in earlier days had submitted to David (2 Sam. 10 ff), not for the ᵓngagements it had conducted continually to gain control over the region of Gilead (Jud. 10:6 ff; 11:4 ff), but for the atrocious manner in which it had handled the latter's population. The Ammonites probably profited by the incursions of the Syrians to the north when they penetrated into the south country. They intended to remain in control of the terrain they had conquered by all means at their disposal. *'They have ripped up women with child in Gilead, that they might enlarge their border'* (v. 13c; cf. also 2 Kgs. 8:12; 15:16). The political motive behind these ghastly measures is clearly unmasked. In attacking the mothers of the next generation it was the future of the Israelites who lived in Gilead that Ammon called in question. It was their way of making sure of keeping the upper hand over the region.

Yahweh does not pardon this attack on human life and this kind of genocide of a nation. He announces that he *'will kindle a fire in the wall of Rabbah'* and in her strongholds (v. 14a). The king himself (certain Greek versions have read here the name of the god of the Ammonites, *Milkom*, for *Malkam* 'their king' in Hebrew) and the court will be deported (v. 15). The manner in which Amos expresses himself here renders transparent the indignation of the God of Israel (v. 14b). Upon Ammon he will hurl himself like a tempest (Jer. 23:19; Ezek. 13:13), and his war-cry (Jer. 4:19; Amos 2:2) will be heard on the day of battle. Yahweh is thus dealing with what we might call a holy war on the wretch who has dared to lay hands on the very sources of life.

(f) Against Moab (2:1–3)

In a quite normal strophe Amos denounces the crime of the people whose ancestor was Ammon (Gen. 19:30 ff), and announces their punishment. Moab has *'burned to lime the bones of the king of Edom'* (2:1c). It is difficult to be precise about the nature of this evil deed, but it must refer to a sacrilegious act against the remains of an Edomite king. Cremation seems to have been an exceptional practice in Israel; death by fire was reserved for great criminals (Gen. 38:24). But Amos was undoubtedly thinking of something

19

else, the profanation of a royal tomb when someone removed the bones from it to turn them into lime. That was an act equivalent to the total liquidation of the deceased, and as such was contrary to the tradition of the Old Testament. (Deut. 21:22 f; 2 Kgs. 9:10, 34 ff).

For this unforgivable deed against a human being, Moab will pay by death. They had employed fire against their enemy, so they would discover fire right within their strongholds (v. 2a). They would lose their rulers—*shophet* here is the equivalent of king—in the course of a disaster that Amos once again pictures as a military action.

Amos is alluding here to an event well-known to his hearers, but of which we know nothing. What is most remarkable in this oracle is the fact that it does not concern itself directly with Israel. It is about the attitude of a foreign nation (Moab) towards another foreign nation (Edom). Yet the God of Israel considers he has the right to intervene, even though his own people are not directly involved, just because a crime has been committed that he simply cannot tolerate. In this strophe Yahweh openly appears as the guardian of a rule which must be observed even by those peoples who do not know his Name.

(g) Against Judah (2:4–5)

This brief strophe on the southern kingdom strikes us as being in contrast both with what precedes and what follows. It keeps to generalities in using a vocabulary familiar from the Deuteronomic writers (the terms *torah*, *hoq* (in the plural), the verb *shamar*, the expression *'to walk after'*, that is to say, to serve, render worship to). This text could only have been written towards the end of the kingdom of Judah and within the framework of the tradition inaugurated by Deuteronomy. Nonetheless, Yahweh has something for which to reproach the Judeans: their infidelity towards the teaching of Yahweh (*torah*, direction, teaching given by the priests and later on the Law). This infidelity is manifested concretely by a refusal to obey his commandments (*shamar*, keep, put into practice), and because of idolatrous practices (*kazab*, a lie, from which comes imposture, an allusion to the false gods who exercise their seductive attraction on the people of Yahweh), or from the example of their fathers who ever so often had served other gods (Deut. 4:3; Jud. 2:12, 19; 1 Kgs. 11:4 ff). Judah could continue to exist only if she remained in touch with her God; if the contrary happened, then even Jerusalem would be consigned to the flames (2:5; cf. 2 Kgs. 25:8–10).

(h) Against Israel (2:6–16)

The strophe is joined to the preceding collection, having basically the same construction, but showing original developments that underline its importance, particularly when the prophet stressed at length the crimes of the Israelites to the north (vv. 6–8). Against the expectation of Jeroboam II's subjects, who see in the condemnation of their neighbours the dawn of a new era of prosperity for Israel, the prophet now identifies the crimes of the Israelites: '*They sell the righteous for silver, and the needy for a pair of shoes*' (v. 6b–c).

We should note that Israel's guilt lies in the social realm, not the religious or the political. Amos will keep on returning to this point (2:7 f; 5:7, 10; 6:12, etc.). The righteous (*tsaddiq*) denotes the innocent, as opposed to the guilty, the equivalent here of the poor (*ebyon*). Compare also later on the word *dal*, or again the plural term *anawim* (v. 7; 5:11 f, etc.).

We should note also the importance of the vocabulary on 'poverty' in Amos' message. The *poor* denote those in Israel who, one way or another, are deprived and whose rights therefore risk being held in contempt; those whose status is called in question, not only in the economic realm, but also in the social, and finally in the cultural and religious realms as well. In consequence these can be manipulated like mere objects by those who hold the power. The divine Law protects the poor (Exod. 23:3, 6, 11; Deut. 15:1 ff; Lev. 19:9 ff; etc.). The sages remind us that they are God's creatures (Prov. 14:31; 19:17; 22:22 f; etc.). All the prophets take up their defence (Isa. 1:17; Jer. 7:6; Micah. 3:1 ff; etc.). The Psalms sing of the ties which bind them to the God of Israel (Pss. 9; 10; 13; 19; etc.). In a word the whole of the Scriptures hail them as 'clients', that is to say, as *the friends of Yahweh*, to whom joy is promised (Isa. 29:19; 41:17; 61:1 ff; and the Beatitudes, Matt. 5:3 ff).

But in spite of the declarations of God's witnesses, the innocent person does not weigh heavily at the judgment when he is without support. The judges allow themselves to be bought (5:12); they sentence the poor to be sold for '*a pair of shoes*' that is, for practically nothing (Gen. 14:23: 1 Sam. 12:3 ff, according to some Greek manuscripts). The expression can also bear a juridical sense to indicate a transaction (Ruth 4:7), in which case Amos would be denouncing the rapacity of some Israelite business men who refrained from nothing since 'business is business'. Verse 7a confirms the fact that, in Jeroboam II's kingdom, the interest of the influential took precedence over the rights of the little people.

21

Justice was scouted, equality was trampled on, to the detriment of the weakest members of Israel. The Hebrew text reads *shaaph*, to aspire to, to covet. This verb is sometimes confused with *shup*, to trample on, as the various versions have understood it. The prophet may have made play with the assonance of the two roots. The desire to get rich at any price leads to the trampling by the rich on the 'little ones'.

We note here that Amos agrees with Israel's juridical tradition, though he does not cite any legal texts; rather he draws his inspiration freely from the traditions that go back to the origins of his people and notably to several passages in the 'Covenant Code' (Exod. 20:22–23:33). See Exod. 21:7–11; Deut. 15:12 ff; Lev. 19:9–37; etc.

Verse 7b, according to some commentators, seems to refer to widespread practice in the Canaanite world and one which the Israelites were only too inclined to adopt—*sacred prostitution*. But Amos, unlike Hosea, does not worry about the religious syncretism that threatens Israel. His message is concentrated on the social disorder that was the rule in Samaria and in the countryside. He denounces a violation of family rights (Exod. 21:7–11; Deut. 22:29 ff) that protected a young girl from the arbitrary behaviour of her master. It is a kind of 'residential prostitution' that Amos castigates here. A servant-girl must not be betrayed to the sexual appetites of a father and his son. Dealing with a female slave in this way was equivalent to profaning the holiness of Yahweh. This passage underlines, as do other texts (Lev. 18:17; 20:14; etc.) the seriousness of sexual relations within the bosom of a single family.

Verse 8 attacks another abuse of the Israelites. Among them were individuals who used goods taken in pledge as if they were their own property, even for religious purposes. The Law actually saw to it that an insolvent debtor must hand over his cloak to his creditor; but it adds that if this is the only covering the poor creature has, then he must receive it back before the sun goes down (Exod. 22:25 f; Deut. 24:12 f, 17); for in the eyes of Yahweh the existence of a human life is more precious than any payment of a debt.

Amos observes that a favoured class profits from its situation by extorting another's goods. In that case its attitude is doubly blameworthy, bacause it is accompanied by a veneer of piety. An iniquity, even when it reaches into cultic practice, remains an iniquity!

We note that every case brought to light by the prophet points to a violation of social justice, that is to say, to the oppression of a weaker person by one who has withheld his aid. But Yahweh requires that the strong should come to the aid of his deprived neighbour. The upper classes of Samaria showed their contempt for those they regarded as 'the poor', and in doing so showed their contempt for the God who was their God. 'To outrage a man is to outrage God who stands behind him. This is what was to be so plainly revealed by the cross of Golgotha' (S. Amsler). There is no service of God independent of service to one's neighbour (cf. Matt. 25:31 ff). The 'Summary of the Law' strictly unites love for God (Deut. 6:4 f) with love of neighbour (Lev. 19:18; cf. Mark 12:28 ff). The prophets each in their own way remind us of this (Hos. 6:6; Micah. 6:8; Amos 5:21 ff). Despite being so magnificent, the kingdom of Jeroboam II was to disappear for neglecting this truth so evident in Yahweh's Revelation.

To emphasise the guilt of the Israelites, Amos opposes their behaviour towards the 'little ones' with that of Yahweh towards them (vv. 9–12). He begins with the words, 'Yet I' (v. 9a, repeated at v. 10a), and accompanies them by a series of verbs in the first person singular: '*I destroyed*', '*I brought up*', '*I raised up*'. In this paragraph, which some exegetes regard as having been added by later editors, though no conclusion has been reached in the matter, the prophet lists the divine interventions in Israel's favour. We are in the presence of a kind of 'historical credo' (G. von Rad) that is a résumé of the Yahwistic faith (cf. also Deut. 26:5 ff; Josh. 24:2 ff; Ps. 136; etc.). Amos begins by referring to an event in which the inhabitants of the northern kingdom were directly interested, that of the complete destruction of the Amorites—'*his fruit above, and his roots beneath*' (v. 9c)—that is to say, of all the Canaanites. The prophet insists on the extraordinary strength of these native peoples, attested by their tall stature (Num. 13:32 f; Deut. 2:10; etc.); but says that they could do nothing against Yahweh. Then he recalls that their destruction was not at the hands of the Israelites, proud of their military successes as they were, but uniquely at the hands of their God. Israel was thus living in a land that she had not conquered herself but which she had been given by Yahweh who remained its Lord. She could thus be destroyed just as her predecessors had experienced.

Amos then recalls elements in the history of the people of Yahweh. He points to the exodus from Egypt (3:1; 9:7) and to the long march across the desert (the symbolical figure of forty years suggests a complete period, the equivalent of a whole generation—cf. also Amos 5:25; Exod. 16:35; Num. 14:33 f; etc.). We should note that, beginning from v. 10, there is a change of person. Amos addresses his brethren in the north directly, (*you, your* sons, *your* young men).

23

These initial interventions presuppose still others, such as Yahweh's accompanying the tribes of Israel up to the present historical moment, in that the God of Israel had raised up prophets and Nazirites (v. 11; Jer. 2:6; Exod. 14:30 f). Amos demonstrates here that Yahweh's activity on behalf of his own was not finished with the settlement in Canaan. The presence of his witnesses in Israel's midst proved that. The prophet is perhaps thinking of Moses (Hos. 12:10, 13), of Elijah (I Kgs. 17 ff), of Micaiah (1 Kgs. 22). As for the Nazirites, a late legal text gives their status (Num. 6:1 ff): it concerns the man or the woman who has vowed himself wholly to Yahweh, either for life (1 Sam. 1:28), or for a limited period (Num. 6:5f). He or she has to abstain from all intoxicating liquor, and all contact with a dead person; and he is not to shave throughout the period of his 'separation'. Hair was then often considered to be endowed with a special power that gave strength and therefore was subject to certain prohibitions. Does Amos think here of Samson (Jud. 13:1 ff), or of other Judges who intervened on Israel's behalf? Anyway he brutally summons the Israelites (v. 11b) and then reminds them of the stupid and impious manner in which they had behaved themselves towards the witnesses whom their God had given them (v. 12). Their attitude was witness of their ingratitude and of their rebellion against Yahweh.

Verses 13 ff, describe the consequences of the behaviour of the Israelites. Amos proclaims Yahweh's judgment on the people by God himself, who announces in a particularly solemn manner: *'Behold, I will . . .'* The divine intervention is linked to the verb *'uq*, which appears only here, and which the Versions translate in various ways, such as 'to roll', 'to crackle', 'to press'. Specialists have sought its meaning from other Semitic roots, such as to stagger, to split open, to tear up. These suggest the soil cracking, or a chariot heavily laden and stuck in the mud. The best solution consists in linking this verb with the earthquake announced already in Amos 1:2, and often cited under one form or another in the prophet's message (3:14 f; 4:11; 6:11; 8:8; 9:1). The earth splits open from the effect of a cataclysm under the feet of the Israelites who will sink into it, much like a cart crushed beneath the weight of the harvested grain that it is transporting. Yahweh's intervention throws panic into the Israelites' ranks, as when a military disaster occurs (vv. 14 ff). It becomes a general 'each one save himself'. Each one seeks safety in flight, but in vain. The bravest and the swiftest are in confusion; warriors, bowmen, infantrymen, and horsemen (vv. 14c–15c) lose their lives. We note the deliberate repetition of the same terms and the panting rhythm of this strophe. The most valiant of all will flee away naked, that is to say, without anything to protect them on the day when Yahweh will chastise his people (v. 16). This poem comes to its climax with a vision of collapse and of panic. So disappeared the troops of Jeroboam II, who had been the glory of their land.

This poem, whose conclusion must have upset and scandalized Amos' hearers, because they were the first to be noted by the prophet, left them no more hope of salvation than it did the nations around the northern kingdom. He thus makes it clear that Yahweh is not a national deity, egoist and partial, interested only in the prosperity of his own and in the crushing of their enemies, as had at times been maintained. The God of Israel watches over the whole group of peoples that occupied the region of Syro-Palestine, those who had been to a certain extent in contact with him when David imposed his authority over them. He reproaches these states, not for making war or even for trading in slaves, but for their inexpressible cruelty to the unfortunate populations that they had conquered. He condemns their furious destructiveness and passion to humiliate, their unmerciful suppression of all hope for the future of a country occupied by their troops, their obliteration without trace of their adversaries to the extent of burning their bones. It is this *total war* that Yahweh cannot accept; and for having ignored this fact, Damascus, Gaza and others like them are to be the prey of the fire that they have themselves lit against others. Amos is not referring here to any identified universal ethical principle placed under the divine authority as was thought at the beginning of this century. He is not invoking the 'Noahic covenant' (Gen. 9), which binds together the totality of the nations, as Rabbi A. Neher (1950) would see it. He lays the stress perhaps more simply upon the existence of a kind of code of conduct or of international law that is taken for granted and which is meant to cover the behaviour of the political powers towards each other, especially in the case of conflict, as J. Barton presumes. Amos affirms above all that the authorities must not give themselves over to any kind of abuse in the name of state rights; for, just as 'the poor' in Israel remain Yahweh's protegees, so the populations of the region, despite their misdeeds and their misery, remain human beings who are not beyond the solicitude of the God of Israel.

PART II

ORACLES AGAINST THE NORTHERN KINGDOM AND AGAINST ITS 'ELITE'

Amos 3:1–6:14

The prophet's accusations in chapters 3 to 6 do not offer the same formal unity as they do in the first part of this collection. They give the impression of being simply juxtaposed the one next to the other without any special order. Consequently at times one feels that they should each be handled separately and independently of their context. A more careful examination of these texts, however, brings to view that the editors of Amos' book did not assemble his prophetic speeches fortuitously, rather they sought to present them with a degree of coherence even when their plan sometimes escapes us. It is observable, for example, that three of the collections of oracles begin with the same word-order. The latter then presents a pressing invitation to the listener, just as to the reader, to take seriously what Amos is saying: '*Hear this word* . . .' (3:1; 4:1; 5:1). A certain analogy too is noticeable in the construction of chapters 3 and 4. More arguments of this nature could be produced.

Amos 3:1–2   Chosen and Judged

This short oracle portrays one of the most important, and for some persons the most disconcerting, aspect of the biblical revelation, that of God's election of Israel (cf. the echo of it in the N.T., in Rom. 9–11). The specific term for this, the verb *bahar*, is not used by Amos. We meet with it particularly in Deuteronomy and in Deutero-Isaiah; for it is when the exile is looming, at the moment when Israel is menaced with death, physically and spiritually, as well as after the disaster of 587, that the theme of 'the chosen people' takes on a position of decisive importance.

But the idea that God would choose for himself a man (thus, Abraham, in Gen. 12:2 f; 18:19, where the verb *yada*' occurs), or a nation (thus, Exod. 19:3–8), comes from before the period that saw the end of the kingdoms of Israel and Judah. Hosea bears witness to it (Hos. 11:1; 13:5; etc.), as Amos does, when he lets us understand in this passage that the election of Israel is a reality, a ·datum readily admissible by those with whom Amos is in dialogue. The verb the prophet actually employs here is *yada'*, which means to know personally, to distinguish, to love; whence also, as the occasion arises, to choose, to elect: '*You only have I known . . .*' (3:2a). He is not proclaiming a new truth to his listeners who have found his observations too severe, and who cannot imagine that Yahweh would ever smite them since they constituted his own people. Amos 3:2a thus probably echoes a polemic aroused by Amos' intrusion.

The prophet's declaration is made up of two elements, with an introduction (v. 1a,b), rather extended and which some commentators suppose either as a whole or in part to be the work of later editors; and v. 2 which can be divided into two. Verse 2a refers to a fact, the election of Israel, and v. 2b deduces its consequences. The prophet does not elaborate on this; he takes for granted in the case of the Israelites that from amongst the masses of the families of the earth—an allusion to the patriarchal tradition (Gen. 12:3; 28:14)—Yahweh has selected Israel (v. 2a). But from that he draws a conclusion diametrically opposed to that of his partners in dialogue. The latter take it for granted that their election protects them from the divine wrath, and shelters them from the menace of destruction. As for the prophet, it is precisely because the Israelites are the object of Yahweh's choice that he will require them to give an explanation of their iniquities (v. 2b). Just being the people of God offers no absolute guarantee, rather it confers a special responsibility—'*It is you only whom I have "chosen" . . . therefore I will punish you for all your iniquities*'. We are to note the astonishing reversal accomplished by Amos: election (v. 2a) takes the place here of the bill of indictment. We can conceive just how scandalized his hearers must have been by his proposition: the prophet had turned the history of salvation into a history of judgment.

Amos 3:3–8   *Yahweh's Irresistible Summons*

It was probably in response to this negative reaction of the Israelites that Amos felt himself obliged to justify his passing judgment. He does so in the manner of the Wisdom writers by conjuring up a series of observations with which his contemporaries could do nothing but agree (vv. 3–6), leading to the conclusion that since Yahweh has spoken, it is absolutely necessary that someone (Amos himself) should prophesy in his name (v. 8b). Verse 8b is actually the goal of the prophet's utterance, and not v.

6, as is sometimes said. Yet we cannot found a whole doctrine on the affirmation contained in v. 6b. Amos shares with his contemporaries the conviction that every event that takes place on earth comes to pass from the God of Israel. As for v. 7 being in prose, it may well be a marginal note inspired by the Deuteronomic school, and intended to underline the direct links that unite Yahweh and the prophets in general.

In face of the attitude of his adversaries, Amos counter-attacks by posing a series of questions whose answers are evident. He begins with one fact that supposes or provokes another, so that the one is directly connected to the other. With great competency—we can only admire the structure of this piece, especially vv. 4 ff—the prophet plays on the relation between cause and effect. Two men walk together, which means that they had first met; no one can deny that! (v. 3). (The Septuagint has read for 'made an appointment', *ya'ad*, 'know each other', *yada'*.) A lion roars because he has taken his prey (v. 4a); a bird falls onto the ground because of the snare that is there (v. 4a); or again, the sound of a trumpet, which was used for war, sows only trouble in a city (v. 6b); the lion's roar produces fear in the countryside (v. 8a). Conclusion: the fact that Yahweh has spoken had the immediate consequence that a prophet has arisen in the land. Amos here defends his ministry and at the same time suggests that, since he has intervened, it is Yahweh himself who has decided to speak forth his word. Thus people must take seriously the presence in the northern kingdom of Yahweh's witness.

In this utterance in the Wisdom style attention is drawn to the polemical and apologetic aspect of his words; but it must be added that there is also a threat in Amos' declaration. The examples he chooses are almost wholly in the negative, in the sense that they conjure up such things as the chase, war and misfortune. It is not without intent that Amos speaks of a young lion capturing its prey (v. 4b), of a net erected to capture a bird (v. 5b), of the noise of war (v. 6a), of the evil that befalls a city (v. 6b). Moreover the voice of Yahweh becomes confused with the roar of a lion (v. 8; cf. 1:2); it can announce only catastrophe. The cases cited by the prophet also appear to warn the Israelites and to create in them a feeling of insecurity, nay even terror. The prophet's whole message of death is contained implicitly in this discussion on the legitimacy of his activity in the northern kingdom.

Amos 3:9–11 Confusion in Samaria

In this oracle the Hebrew version produces some problems for us that have led commentators to correct the text here and there.

Amos turns to the capital, or more exactly to the ruling class in Samaria. His utterance is shaped like a word of judgment. It is composed of two elements, (a) a denunciation of the Israelites' criminal attitude (vv. 9bf), and (b) a condemnation of the guilty introduced by the word 'therefore' (*laken*, v. 11).

What is of particular significance here is that the prophet assumes the function of a herald, charged with summoning together witnesses who are to be present at the trial that Yahweh is conducting against Samaria. There are to be two such witnesses, as the juridical tradition of Israel demands (Deut. 17:6). Yet the surprising and scandalous fact for Amos's listeners is that these are foreigners. The one comes from Ashdod. (The Septuagint has read *in Assyria,* a variant which has been retained by several exegetes including the RSV; but we should recall that Amos never mentions this country in any of his utterances.) The other comes from Egypt. These two nations are the witnesses against Israel when she is brought to trial by her own God. She is at fault and must be punished.

Verses 9b–10 establish Samaria's guilt. A terrible confusion reigns within it (Ezek. 22:5; Zech. 14:3). In actuality the city is handed over to arbitrariness and becomes the victim of all kinds of deeds of violence. In clear terms Amos denounces the oppression that raged in Samaria in the time of Jeroboam II. This apparently glorious reign actually concealed an intolerable situation. The city had lost all sense of integrity (*nekohah*, 'to know how to do right', v. 10a: note its assonance with *betokah*, 'in her midst' v. 9b), and treasures were accumulated in its palaces, the fruit of violence and robbery (v. 10b). We should note that the word 'palace' (RSV *stronghold*) keeps appearing in this short fragment showing that the prophet envisages the rulers of the country, the court, the high functionaries and the rich merchants. These all are primarily responsible for the chaos reigning in Samaria and are to be judged by their peers from Ashdod and Egypt. Equally we are to note the importance of the vocabulary of oppression appearing in this passage: the verb *'ashaq,* which pictures the idea of exploitation, the nouns *hamas* and *shod,* which express the ideas of violence and brutality.

The great ones of Samaria, Amos notes ironically, have finally accumulated only violence and plunder, and these will be of no protection to them in the hour of punishment (v. 11). The enemy will encircle the land—which one is not mentioned expressly—the strength of Samaria will fall to pieces and its treasures will pass to the invader. Those who have pillaged will be pillaged in their turn!

Amos 3:12ab   *Witnesses of Israel's Death*

Verse 12, from which we should probably detach the last line, v. 12c, and which may be read instead along with what follows, constitutes a unique unity. It is a kind of parable that rests upon a juridical tradition attested in Israel (Exod. 22:9–12) and found in the Code of Hammurabi (no. 266). Its purpose is certainly not to provide the prophet's hearers with a note of consolation, revealing to them that some of the inhabitants of Samaria will escape the judgment. There is no need to speculate on the notion of a 'remnant', for this does not play any positive role with Amos, even though it has often been attributed to him. The prophet's utterance is best understood if we approach it from the standpoint of the ruling that requires the shepherd to bring back to his master proof that the beast that has disappeared from the flock has really been mangled by a lion and not simply stolen by him (Exod. 22:12; Gen. 31:39; 1 Sam. 17:34 f). The words *'As the shepherd rescues from the mouth of the lion two legs, or a piece of an ear'* (3:12a) witness to the disappearance of a sheep without his guardian being held responsible; so then (3:12b) a handful of Israelites, plucked (using the same verb, *natsal*) from the catastrophe, will attest to the end of the kingdom of Jeroboam II, without the blame being attributed to God! The escapees will serve as exhibits and their presence as proof of the annihilation of a guilty nation. Amos does not announce the coming *in extremis* of a salvation designed to 'neutralize' the divine judgment, he demands that the Word of Yahweh (v. 12a) should be taken seriously.

Amos 3:12c–15   *Against Samaria's Luxurious Homes*

This chapter's final pericope poses some difficult questions. These have inspired numerous hypotheses on the part of various commentators. Its heavy style makes us feel it is overloaded. Particularly v. 12c poses problems that are almost insurmountable. This line might be joined with what precedes it, in which case it is the ending of v. 12ab, or it might go with what follows. In that case it concerns the inhabitants of Samaria, and in particular it is those who were living in a state of luxury. This luxury rests upon their iniquitous behaviour. The attitude of the people of Samaria who are being summoned by the prophet (v. 12c) and who are being called to witness against the house of Jacob, that is to say, against Israel itself (v. 13), betrays their taste for ostentation and their greed for possessions. They sprawl on divans and acquire houses that they inhabit only seasonally and these they decorate sumptuously (v. 15). However, the last words of v. 12c are obscure.

31

It seems that the inhabitants of the capital loved to stretch themselves on soft couches: *'with the corner of a couch'*, and *'part of a bed'* is a possible translation but one which remains conjectural. The Versions actually see a reference here to Damascus (and so to the English word 'damask') a solution adopted by more than one translator, but which presupposes a reading different from the Hebrew text. We shall have to be content with a translation that is only approximate while admitting that the prophet, as at 6:1 ff, is denouncing the easy-going ways and the pursuit of comfort on the part of Samaria's rulers. After the summons comes the announcement of punishment (vv. 14 f). Yahweh is about to conduct an attack upon the religious centre of the northern kingdom (v. 14) and on what constitutes the glory of the leaders of the state—their rich homes (v. 15). The prophet means here the sanctuary at Bethel, a fact which a note at v. 14b makes explicit. He indicates that on the day when God will render the account to his people every source of security will be removed; the horns of the altar, pledge of the right of asylum where even the guilty can find refuge if he but seizes hold of them (Exod. 21:12–14; 1 Kgs. 1:50; 2:28), shall be smashed just as the winter and summer houses, covered over as they are with ivory, shall collapse in ruins, smitten by Yahweh. In excavations made in Samaria ivory decorations have turned up revealing that the rich loved to decorate their various residences.

We should note the part played by the God of Israel in this catastrophe. He devastates like an earthquake. Amos keeps pursuing this idea. Thus he ends this chapter 3, as he did the preceding one, with a vision of ruin. Everything on which the pride of Israel built its security has been removed. God's 'visit' (from the verb *paqad*, to visit, to inspect, whence to call to account, to punish) evoked at the beginning just as at the end of this collection (3:2, 14) signifies in a concrete way a catastrophe without precedent for the northern kingdom.

Amos 4

This chapter begins with a summons as do 3:1 and 5:1, and concludes with a portrayal of Yahweh's irresistible might (v. 13). Israel must now get ready to meet it (v. 12), since she has paid no attention to the warnings which her God has offered her (vv. 6 ff). The chapter is composed of three elements: (a) an oracle of judgment upon the great ladies of the city (vv. 1–3); (b) a kind of parody upon priestly instruction (vv. 4 f); (c) a long pericope exhibiting a rhythmical refrain (vv. 6b, 8b, 9b, 10b, 11b), which concludes with the announcement of a final confrontation between

Yahweh and his own people (vv. 6–13). Commentators disagree about the relationship between these various passages. Some handle them separately; others connect them, as W. Brueggemann has done. He suggests that vv. 4–13 should be put back in a context that has to do with the Covenant, since they constitute a sort of renewal of the liturgy of the *berit* (covenant). But this hypothesis clashes with the fact that the Covenant plays almost no role in Amos' message.

Amos 4:1–3   *Against the Great Ladies of Samaria*

In this utterance the prophet censures the women of the capital (v. 1a), ardently exposing their faults (v. 1b–c). He introduces in a particularly solemn manner (v. 2a) the announcement of their punishment (vv. 2bf).

The general effect of the passage is clear, even if some details remain odd and obscure. This is so in the case of 4:2, where we hear of ropes, hooks, baskets, harpoons etc: these all indicate that we do not know the precise form that the execution of the judgment upon the guilty will take. Some specialists would like to see in this oracle an allusion to the fertility cults; but it is clear that Amos, here and elsewhere, is dealing on the social plane, as is indicated by his choice of words dealing with poverty, humiliation and impotence, as well as those dealing with the oppression and destruction that we find in v. 1.

Amos summons the ladies of the capital with severity, but in referring to them as '*cows of Bashan*', he is not actually insulting them as people have sometimes supposed. The territory of Bashan, on the other side of the Jordan, was known for its rich pasturage (Jer. 50:19; Micah. 7:14) and for the quality of its flocks (Deut. 32:14; Ezek. 39:18). So the prophet emphasises the weight of the women of Samaria—to be fat was to share in the oriental idea of beauty—and so expresses their importance at the same time. He has to deal with women of quality; but that renders their attitude all the more unacceptable. They have only scorn for those whom they are exploiting and think only of their own pleasure. Their husbands—Amos styles them ironically '*your lords*' (as the Hebrew means)—must just bow before their caprices. '*Bring, that we may drink!*' Such is the command that crosses lips of these beautiful ladies! Truly licentiousness reigns in Samaria (3:9).

The punishment will be in proportion to these shameful deeds (vv. 2bf). These 'high-born ladies' will be seen to depart one after the other, through breaches in the walls of a town in ruins, one that has been destroyed by an enemy, or perhaps by some form of earth tremor. But they will not go out as free women, neither they nor their servants, nor their offspring (*aharitken*, those who come after you, who are behind you; others translate the same word by 'their bottoms'!). They will be led, like obstreperous beasts goaded by blows (or, according to other commentators, with hooks). They will be dragged away like long files of prisoners, bound to each other by chains bored through the nose, such as one can see in Assyrian reliefs. Other translations again suggest that the women of Samaria, or their dead bodies, will be carried out with hooks or pruning-hooks.

If the details of the punishment of the grand ladies of Samaria are not clear to us, it is certain that the prophet reserves for them a fate both humiliating and painful. They are to be led off with blows from steel-tipped clubs, packed together like sardines, or chained like captives. Thus they will be driven or transported in the direction of Hermon (according to the Greek), which marks the northern limit of the northern kingdom on the other side of the Jordan. So Amos hints here perhaps (v. 3) that the female inhabitants of Samaria will be deported (Amos 5:27).

Amos' harshness should be noted. He conjures up visions of horror such as have become only too familiar in our own century. Through his words we understand the indignation of Yahweh himself against the exploitation of those who are the weakest members of society.

Amos 4:4–5   Sacrilegious Worship

According to Jer. 18:18 it was the task of the priest to convey instruction (*torah*, the Law); but a prophet could occasionally communicate a *torah*. This is just what Amos does here (cf. also 5:4 ff, 14 f, 24). He quite simply recalls his contemporaries to the divine will and places their responsibilities before them.

What is astonishing here is the paradoxical, even scandalous nature of the prophet's utterance. Amos exhorts his hearers, assembled probably in Bethel, one of the most prestigious sanctuaries of the northern kingdom, to betake themselves to the temple in order to commit more and more sin, '*Come and transgress*'. In this way he assimilates the worship that the Israelites offered to Yahweh with an act of rebellion against their God, and he places the whole range of the rites that they observe under the one condemnation.

Now, for the inhabitants of the northern kingdom, to gather at Bethel or at Gilgal was a normal activity and was part of the spiritual life that justified the historical and religious importance in particular of the Sanctuaries to be found there. Bethel, besides being the official centre of the cult of the kingdom of Israel,

following upon the measures taken by Jeroboam I (1 Kgs. 12:26 ff),
was actually bound up with a memory of the patriarchs and
particularly of Jacob (Gen. 12:8; 13:3; 28:10 ff). As for Gilgal, it lay
near Jericho and preserved the traditions that centered around the
crossing of the Jordan and the beginnings of the occupation of
Canaan (Josh. 1:4 f). It had played a decisive role too at the
commencement of kingship (1 Sam. 11:14 f; 13:4 ff; 15:12 ff, etc.).
Bethel and 'the' Gilgal appeared therefore in the eyes of the
Israelites as venerable spots bound to the cult of Yahweh—places
where his people loved to assemble.

Amos throws himself into an attack not only on these
sanctuaries, but also on the various rites that had been practised in
them for generations (vv. 4b f)—blood sacrifices every morning
that became a communion feast; the bringing of tithes on the third
day of the festival (Gen. 28:22); offering sacrifices of thanksgiving
with leavened bread, something which was forbidden by the
priestly law later on (Lev. 2:4 f, 11 f; 7:12); then freewill offerings.
What is striking about this insult made by the prophet is the
liberality of the Israelites, the zeal of their religious practices, the
super-abundance of their rites and of their offerings. Yahweh ought
to be fully satisfied with the cult carried on equally at Bethel and at
Gilgal.

Now, according to Amos, it is quite the contrary. His remarks
must have astonished and then shocked his hearers. Once again he
is in total disagreement with them. The prophet does not give
express reasons for Yahweh's negative attitude to the Israelites'
religious ceremonies, but he lets the chief motive appear in his last
words, '*for so you love to do*'. The God of Israel does not reject a
schismatic cult, as has been thought at times. He does not reproach
the officials with performing their service incorrectly by being
disobedient to the Law, as has also been suggested. He notes
simply that the Israelites were delighted with a religious life from
which Yahweh was totally absent. Yahweh has no use for practices
where his people seek their own satisfaction rather than honour
God. It is not by chance that the prophet speaks of 'your' sacrifices,
'your' tithes, 'your' freewill offerings. At Bethel, as at Gilgal, Israel
is only seeking its own pleasure, so Yahweh spurns their
hypocritical rites (Isa. 29:13; Matt. 6:1 ff; 15:1 ff; etc.). It is not
enough just to offer sacrifices and to burn incense, even in ardent
zeal, to make the worship of God into a reality.

Amos 4:6–13   The Israelites' Delusion

This poem, formed of five strophes (vv. 6–11), each one of which
ends with the same refrain, concludes with a threat (v. 12). This is

reinforced by a fragment of a hymn in honour of Yahweh (v. 13). The sense of Amos' utterance is clear: Israel has scorned the warnings her God has given her; she must now meet with his wrath. The prophet testifies here to the blindness of the Israelites, to their inability to seize the chances God has offered them in the past to repent: '*Yet you did not return to me*' (using the verb *shubh*, which serves to express the idea of returning, of conversion, of repentance: vv. 6, 8, 9, etc.).

Amos is here composing a sort of parody upon 'salvation history'. Instead of listing, as the official liturgy seeks to do, Yahweh's interventions on behalf of Israel, he recalls how God has smitten his own, not in order to destroy them, but in order to lead them back to himself. The succession of 'plagues' that he has thrust upon Israel have not attained the end purposed by Yahweh, since the divine appeals have remained without any response. Verses 6–11 thus form a charter of accusations brought against Israel; v. 12 pronounces judgment preceded by the classical formula '*Therefore . . .*' (*laken*); while v. 13 gives the glory to the God that has handled events from beginning to end—'*I gave you . . .*' (v. 6), '*And I also withheld . . .*' (v. 7, etc.). Verses 6 ff. thus constitute a kind of catalogue of the calamities that Israel has known, all of them natural events occurring in the region, such as famine, drought, epidemics or war. So Yahweh has employed both nature and history to warn his people. (We should note that the majority of these 'plagues' are to be found mentioned in the priestly material, such as Lev. 26:29 f; Deut. 28:21 ff; 60 f; etc.)

The first strophe (v. 6) pictures a famine, or more modestly, a dearth ('*cleanness of teeth*'), a phenomenon well known in the near-eastern world. This first 'plague' brings no response, no more do those that follow.

The second strophe (vv. 7–8) develops at length another ordeal, particularly terrible: lack of water. This brings about a drought that affects the fields, the animals and man (Jer. 14). The life of the country especially depends on the rain that Yahweh grants or withholds from his people. Amos conjures up the confusion brought about by Israel's God. The rain falls here, but not there, and the people, in extremities, run in vain from one cistern to another to slake their thirst. The prophet then goes on to picture crowds staggering in search of a drop of water (cf. an echo of this at Amos 8:11 f).

The third strophe (v. 9) speaks of another evil—a blight strikes the vegetation; the orchards and the vineyards that form Israel's glory are wasted. The grain becomes rotten, burnt dry by the east wind, and mildew settles upon it (1 Kgs. 8:37; Hag. 2:17; Deut. 28:22).

The fig trees and the olive trees are devoured by locusts. This all means ruin for the whole population who see their efforts stultified.

The fourth strophe (v. 10) would seem to describe not a massacre ('with the sword' would then be an addition), but an epidemic that this time touches the elite of the nation, the cream of its soldiers. The pestilence, showing itself in their ranks, transforms their camp into a stinking charnel house. The victories of Jeroboam II and of his father (2 Kgs. 14:25, 28) do not shelter the army from such a calamity, one that recalls the last of the Egyptian plagues (Exod. 11:4 ff; 12:29 ff; cf. also 2 Kgs. 19:35).

The fifth strophe (v. 11) reminds one of still another cataclysm, an earthquake. Amos keeps on returning to such a phenomenon, one that took place more frequently than we imagine in his region: it was of such a violent nature that it could be compared with the disaster that destroyed Sodom and Gomorrah (Gen. 19). But no more did this final warning lead Israel back to her God.

Yahweh's patience with his own people has its limits; the hour of judgment has come (v. 12). This verse makes a clear announcement of the judgment upon the guilty, without entering into details. Some exegetes ask themselves whether the event envisaged by the prophet was so horrible that a later editor had altered it, preferring to censor Amos' utterances. That is scarcely probable although this verse is constructed in an unexpected manner. Verse 12c, which seems to repeat v. 12a and 12b, confines itself to declaring *'Prepare to meet your God, O Israel'*. But the condemnation of Israel consists precisely in that she must prepare for a face to face encounter with her God whom she has never ceased to reject. Her worst possible misfortune at this hour is to have direct dealings with Yahweh. Verse 12c is thus not a last appeal to convert, as some think; it says plainly that the time for the settlement of accounts has come. In his own way the prophet anticipates the apostolic word: 'It is a fearful thing to fall into the hands of the living God'! (Heb. 10:31).

Verse 13 specifies the grandeur of this God whose name is Yahweh. The verse comes to us like a fragment of a hymn composed to the glory of the God of Israel. It is similar to other formulas that are attested in the book of Amos (5:8 f; 9:5 f), with which it was possibly connected in origin. The purpose of this verse, which is probably the work of an editor, is, it seems, to declare the grandeur of Yahweh at the very moment he judges the guilty, according to an already ancient hypothesis. (F. Horst). Amos 4:13 thus attests the extraordinary might of the God of Israel, his authority over the universe and his creative power. We should note that this liturgical text by and large uses the vocabulary of creation (form, create, make). It speaks of the power of Yahweh over the mountains and the wind (*ruah*), his superiority over the 'heights' of the earth. The same God reveals his plan to his human creature (*adam*)—we might understand these words as 'He knows the thoughts of man' (Jer. 11:20; Ps. 94:11; etc.). The word *seah*, occurring only here, is comparable with *siah* which means concern, thought, purpose. The Septuagint has read *mah-seho* as if it were *mashiho*, that is to say, as 'his Messiah', thus favouring a christological reading of this passage that had much success with the Fathers of the Church. What strikes us in this confession that ends chapter 4 is the omnipresence of Yahweh, his unceasing activity, his universal sovereignty. It is with such a God then that the Israelites are to meet!

Amos 5

This chapter, which opens with a song of lamentation (vv. 1–3) and ends with a threat of deportation for the Israelites (v. 27), and in which the prophet outlines various misfortunes that will happen to them (thus vv. 16 f and vv. 18 f), is probably the most important in Amos' book. In it we find a list of the characteristic themes arrived at by the prophet such as the trial of Israelite society given over to injustice (particularly vv. 10 ff), the rejection of the worship that Israel offers her God (vv. 21 ff), and the radical calling into question of the Israelites' hope (vv. 18 ff). Once more the prophet adopts the contrary opinion to that of his questioners and turns their most cherished traditions upside down.

This chapter is divisible into four parts: vv. 1–3; 4–17; 18–20; 21–27. Many exegetes have been struck by the lack of order they find in the pericope vv. 4–17. The same ideas keep appearing in different passages; thus vv. 4 ff. are maintained at 14 f., and 7 is connected with vv. 10 ff. However an interesting study by J. de Waard encourages us to look at Amos 5: 1–17 in another light. The editor responsible for this collection may have been employing a structure known as 'chiasmus', that is, a literary form that resembles somewhat an X. This is because the various elements of this piece are organized in such a way that they relate to each other as in the following diagram: a b c c′ b′ a′. According to de Waard vv. 1–3 correspond with 16 ff, vv. 4–6 with vv. 14 f, v. 7 with the pericope vv. 10–12 (13), and so on. The composition of Amos 5:1–17, then, can be represented in this manner (see facing page).

Thanks to de Waard's analysis we can recognize that the central affirmation of this collection is concentrated on the divine name, '*The Lord is his name*' (v. 8d). For the rest, the pericope begins and ends with the theme of death, and Amos' exhortation in vv. 4 ff and

A(vv. 1–3)

       B(vv. 4–6)

            C(v. 7)

                  D(v. 8a, b, c)

                        E(v. 8d *Yahweh shemo*)

                  D'(v. 9)

            C'(vv. 10–12 (13))

       B'(vv. 14 f)

A'(vv. 16 f)

in vv. 14 f precedes the speech for the prosecution against the iniquitous lawsuits now going on in Israel (v. 7 and vv. 10 f). In a word, just there where at first sight there is only disorder, de Waard uncovers a preconceived plan leading on from beginning to end according to a simple and flowing structure.

Amos 5:1–3   *Lamentation over the Destruction of Israel*

This short utterance, placed under the protection of the divine Word, is presented in the form of a song of lament, a *qinah*. Its characteristic rhythm (accentuated 3–2, a 'broken' rhythm) is associated in the Israelite mentality with death, and so, by extension, with all kinds of distress and calamities. On hearing such an elegy Israel would know at once that a disaster has occurred, that death is there. It is for the people themselves that the prophet summons his questioners to weep. He pictures the sad fate of a virgin, forsaken, with no one to come to her help, dying prematurely before she has been able to realize her vocation as wife and mother. The theme of Israel as Yahweh's wife, which was to serve other prophets to illustrate the tumultuous relationship between God and his people (Hos. 2:4 ff; Jer. 2:2 ff, etc.), is only touched on here.

To put it concretely, Amos envisages the destruction of the military power of the northern kingdom (v. 3). Yahweh has actually decided on the near destruction of the army of which the king is so proud, and the tenth of it that will remain will be ineffective. Contrary to the interpretation of some who see in this 'remnant' a consoling note permitting hope for a renewal of Yahweh's people, the prophet here lays stress on the extent of the catastrophe that is about to fall on Israel, and on the impotence to which those who escape are condemned. We must not transform the terrible announcement Amos has made throughout this *qinah* in to a message of salvation!

Amos 5:4–6   *It is Yahweh Himself who must be Sought*

This pronouncement is in imitation of a priestly *torah*. It first lays a command upon the Israelites (v. 4), then a prohibition (v. 5), and then adds some comments by the prophet. Amos conveys a divine speech that once again must have both surprised and exasperated his hearers. Perhaps he is answering an objection on their part.

Amos' opponents probably asserted that they were in fact 'seeking for' Yahweh; they were doing just this because they were assiduously visiting the sanctuaries in the north and even in the south. They considered themselves to be right with God, and were living in the assurance of his blessing. Amos replies by bidding them 'seek the Lord' as if that was not precisely what they were doing! (v. 4). He continues by referring once again to the two venerable spots (v. 5), Bethel and Gilgal, and adds in also Beer-sheba. The latter also lay in Judah; it too guarded the memory of the patriarchal traditions (Gen. 21:33; 26:23 ff; 46:1 ff). The prophet and his opponents are in agreement on one point: it is with Yahweh that life is to be found, with all the riches that that implies; but they diverge about the way one ought to seek the God of Israel. For the Israelites, to seek God meant to offer worship to the nation's divinity, to go on pilgrimage to the holy places, to observe the traditional ritual. For Amos, to seek Yahweh required obedience to his Law, making his will one's own, living in communion with him. In his eyes Israel was only 'making use' of God when it went on pilgrimage, just 'play-acting'. It was not really seeking him. By continuing in that attitude it would not find life, but death (v. 6).

The traditional holy places are condemned. As a skilful orator, and playing with assonances, Amos proclaims that Bethel, ('the house of God'), is destined to become *aven*, 'nothing at all', or 'a place of iniquity' (Hos. 4:15; 10:5, 8), and that 'the' Gilgal is to be completely deported (*wehaggilgal galoh yigeleh*).

Urgently Amos takes up the divine appeal, for he knows that '*the house of Joseph*' (Israel) is threatened with the sight of the wrath of her God '*breaking out like fire*' against her (6). One might ask if the prophet, at the moment of his intervention, is not really placing before his listeners an alternative—the same problem comes up in the case of 5:14 f—life or death; life lived in obedience to Yahweh, or death by persisting in a pseudo-religious attitude that covers over all sorts of crimes. But for him, the die may have been cast, that is to say, the judgment upon Israel is irreversible. In that case the prophetic appeals would serve only to underline the inability of God's people to seek for God at all and to live in his presence. The actual context of the prophetic exhortations in chapter 5 seems to require this second solution—that the condemnation of Israel has been decided already, that her repentance is inconceivable, and that the Israelites set out upon a road that can only lead to catastrophe. It is significant that each of Amos' addresses is found to be accompanied by a mention of deportation or of death.

Amos 5:14–15   Perhaps . . .

On another occasion the prophet picks up and states a former idea more precisely. He speaks now in his own name while employing the form of a priestly *torah.* To seek God (5:4) means concretely to seek good and not evil, to hold to the former and to reject the latter (14a, 15a; Deut. 30:15). It is not a question of the Good in itself, but that which Yahweh demands or condemns. Amos places himself firmly in the Yahwistic tradition. For him, everything is played out within the context of justice and this must be upheld or *'established in the gate'* (v. 15a), in other words at the entrance to the city in the public square where meetings are held, where business affairs are attended to, and where justice is administered. *'The gate'* thus means the court of justice. Amos also reminds the Israelites that the worship of Yahweh must pass through, show itself in, respect for others. In this manner he anticipates the strict relationship established by Jesus between the two commandments that sum up the whole of the divine will (Matt. 22:34 ff).

In his assertions Amos makes allusion to what his hearers are talking about. They then counter-attack the prophet; for he is threatening them with the divine wrath that Yahweh has towards them (v. 14b). They declare that Yahweh is with them and therefore cannot reject them. For the prophet, the presence of God is not unconditional, it depends on the way in which Yahweh's people observe justice in both their public and their private affairs. The fate of Israel, he believes, is determined by their attitude towards justice and is not dependent upon their election. The prophet concludes his oracle by a saying that opens up a possibility of survival for the Israelites, even though a limited one. It rests not on Israel's merits but on divine grace, which Amos takes seriously in spite of the severity of his charge. It has to do only with a 'remnant'. Amos does not announce it as evidence, but only as a hope, employing the word *'perhaps', it may be.* We must not turn this *'perhaps'*, however, into a guarantee given to the people of God that everything will turn out all right for them; their history does not issue in a 'happy ending' but in the cross. In taking seriously the pronouncement of judgment that has by now been so often repeated by God himself against his own people, along with this 'perhaps' uttered by the prophet, we must admit that if God remains faithful to his word now entrusted to Amos, he remains no less its Lord. His grace may grant to Israel, against all expectation, a new possibility of life.

Amos 5:7 and 10–12(13)   Scoffing at the Equity of Justice

Verse 7 is usually linked with vv. 10 ff, as against the RSV, which reads it with v. 6. The text of the Septuagint is quite different and agrees rather with vv. 8 f. It might be possible to regard v. 7 as an introduction to the development of vv. 10 ff, for it seems above all that it is the judges who are responsible for the perversion of justice in Israel. Some exegetes would insert at the head of v. 7 the word *hoy,* that exclamation of anguish that occurs at 5:18 and 6:1. It was in origin a cry of distress such as one uttered at a funeral (1 Kgs. 13:30; Jer. 22:18). We might translate it by the term 'Woe!' Amos places the unrighteous judges under the sign of this ominous woe. He accuses them of having transformed justice into poison (*'wormwood'*). Their judgments are criteria that produce confusion and ruin, for they witness to the contempt in which they hold Yahweh's justice (*tsedaqah*), that which assures the harmony to be found at the heart of the universe and in human society.

At vv. 10 ff the prophet brands the aversion they show towards honest witnesses in a court of law and towards those who stand up for justice. There a man's word plays a decisive role in establishing each person's responsibility (Deut. 17:6 f; 19:16 ff; Prov. 6:19; etc.). Then he goes on to accuse the big landowners for using their position of privilege to despoil the poor of their meagre resources, particularly in putting pressure upon the country folk and in laying seizure to their tenancies. Their intention is clear, they are building themselves luxury homes, are planting the choicest of vines; but the law of the talon, the *lex talionis*, would apply to them: '*The spoilers will be despoiled*' (S. Amsler). The mighty landowners are not to enjoy the fruits of their violence. At v. 12 the prophet concludes by recalling the numerous crimes of those who, having the power, yet abused it, by over-burdening the innocent (*tsaddiq*). They extorted bribes, and '*turned aside the needy*', although the latter are always in the hands of Yahweh (Prov. 14:31; 17:5).

Amos 5:16–17   The Deadly Fruits of Injustice

This speech by Amos completes in a startling manner the case that he directs at the northern kingdom's propertied class: their contempt for justice leads to death. Throughout the whole land there shall be only cries of anguish and mourning rites (8:10). Everyone will share in the mourning, the professionals in funeral lamentations and even, what an acme of irony, the peasants who are the victims of the big landowners.

Amos is perhaps envisaging a natural catastrophe that is about to strike the region or else an invasion. He does not specify which, because the essential for him is the fact that Yahweh himself is about to take measures against his people: '*I will pass through the midst of you*' (v. 17b). This expression reminds us of the last plague in Egypt, the most dreadful of all (Exod. 12:12, 23), only this time it is the people of God who are to be its victim.

Amos 5:8–9   *A Fragment of a Hymn*

This passage, whose contents call to mind a hymn in honour of Yahweh, is introduced into chapter 5 in rather an odd manner. Like 4:13 and 9:5 f it recalls to mind the greatness of God with which both Amos' hearers and readers are confronted. It follows here upon a threatening call by the prophet (v. 6), and it precedes his denunciation of the crimes of the Israelites.

Yahweh manifests himself as the Lord of the cosmos. He reigns over nature, he commands the stars (Job. 9:9; 38:31), he turns deep darkness into the morning, and calls for the waters of the sea and pours them out on the earth. Thus he is not only the God who ensures world order, he is equally able to bring about cosmic cataclysms. This last allusion to Yahweh's might, in this particular context, is especially disquieting.

Verse 9 poses some difficult problems. It appears to be secondary and can be understood in various ways. Some specialists see in this passage an allusion to the stars (the Bull, *shor*, Capricorn, *'ez*, the Vintager, *mebatser*). But more usually it is believed that, according to this couplet, Yahweh lays the blame on mighty man and on his self-assurance. He sends destruction, *shod*, pillage, against the strong, *'az*, and against the citadel. If this is the case, then v. 8 would speak of the extraordinary cosmic might of Yahweh, and v. 9 of the manner in which he breaks forth against his pretentious creature!

Amos 5:13   *Silence is Golden*

This is possibly a marginal comment made by a reader of Amos who prudently concludes that the time to which the prophet refers is so evil that it would be better to keep silent about it. He would then be adopting the circumspect attitude characteristic of the Wisdom tradition (Prov. 10:14; 13:3; Eccles. 3:7, etc.).

If it is Amos who is speaking he would perhaps be expressing a secret wish, even though he knows that Yahweh will compel him to speak (3:8; 7:15). He takes up his mission courageously and with resolution, which is to be above all the man of the Word of God.

Amos 5:18–20   The 'Day of the Lord' will not be What you Expect

This utterance by Amos results probably from a new controversy between the prophet and his listeners. Those who reacted against his message of woe did so because they held to the old tradition that a Day of glory was coming to Israel. But once again Amos separates himself from his contemporaries. 'The Day of the Lord whose coming you desire so ardently (the verb employed by the prophet has a negative connotation, it refers to coveting, Num. 11:34; 2 Sam. 23:15) will be darkness and not light, that is to say, disaster and not prosperity, catastrophe and not salvation' (vv. 18b, 20). We should note Amos' insistence on this point, again illustrated by the parable of the man who escaped one danger (a lion) only to fall into another (a bear) and who, believing himself to be safe at last at home, finally dies falling into a danger which he has never even noticed (a serpent, v. 19). The prophet could not better express the unavoidable character of the disastrous fate awaiting the Israelites; so that is why for their sakes he bursts forth with that exclamation which is used on the occasion of a funeral, *Hoy!*

Therefore Amos does not contest the existence of a 'Day' of the God of Israel. In that respect he is in agreement with his opponents. But from it he draws a diametrically opposite set of consequences. This passage thus reveals a tradition attested as early as the 8th century with regard to a 'Day of the Lord', for it plays an important role in the predictions of the prophets (Isa. 2:2; 13:6 ff, Zeph. 1:14 ff, etc.). Moreover, it continues even into the message of the New Testament (Luke 17:24; 2 Thess. 2:1, 8; etc.). This Day, generally regarded as a day of darkness, fear and terror, doubtless refers back to the first interventions by the God of Israel, which involve a new and final manifestation of his holiness and glory. Even as the Israelites blissfully await the realization of their very dubious hopes, thanks to their God, Amos reveals to them that in reality a mortal threat is hovering over them.

Amos 5:21–27   If only You would be done with Your Rites and Your Prayers and Make Room for Justice!

This well known utterance of Amos is expressed in teaching form (a) what Israel's God will not countenance (vv. 21–23), (b) what

God demands (v. 24)—all in conjunction with the reflections found at vv. 26 f. The pericope then concludes with a threat clearly aimed at the Israelites (v. 27) in which the utterances of the prophet are so violent that taken together they constitute a kind of oracle of judgment.

As Yahweh's spokesman, Amos' thought is clear, even though some verses (vv. 25 f) pose real difficulties. Yahweh rejects the worship which his people offer him (vv. 21 ff); what he looks for is justice and righteousness. The theme is not new (Amos 4:4 ff; 5:4 ff, 14 f), but the prophet's tone here is particularly severe. Amos calls the whole of Israel's worship life to account. Nothing escapes him—their pilgrimages and solemn assemblies (v. 21), their burnt offerings and cereal offerings (v. 22), even their songs and their prayers (v. 23). The prophet does not denounce the ritual of worship itself, nor does he reproach Israel with the paucity of her offerings; but he expresses Yahweh's disgust at the ceremonies that the people organize in his honour. He requires that in Israel's midst justice should roll down like an inexhaustible river and righteousness should assert its presence like life-giving waters (v. 24).

Like other prophets (Isa. 1:10 ff; Micah 6:6 ff; Jer. 7:1 ff) Amos is not dreaming here of a worship that is purely inward and moral, as has been supposed at times. What he condemns is a piety which is not confirmed by a reverential attitude towards the rights of others. Yahweh rejects an 'alibi-religion'. It is not possible to offer him worship while trampling justice under foot. The Gospel does not contradict this teaching (Matt. 5:21 ff; Mark 11:25; etc.).

Amos' remarks must have appeared monstrous to his contemporaries, for they called in question the whole religious life of the Israelites. Amos rejects a cult that is too rich in ceremony, one that was probably influenced by Canaanite ways; and it was too mercenary, though this was denied day after day by those who, even while they entreated the God of Israel, repressed the poor and violated their lawful rights. We should note the significant contrast between '*your* feasts . . . *your* solemn assemblies . . . *your* offerings . . . .' on the one hand, and '*I* hate . . . *I* take no delight . . . *I* will not accept . . . .' on the other hand. It lets us see how the Israelites were more concerned with religion than with God.

Verses 25 ff produce a number of difficulties. Some people believe that they constitute a late addition in prose, as the RSV suggests. Other commentators cut out vv. 25–26 from the original oracle and regard v. 27 as the natural sequel to v. 24, in that, after having rejected the Israelites' cultic practices, Amos would then be giving them notice that they were to be deported.

Verse 25 consists of a rhetorical question whose content is astonishing. Amos seems to be denying the existence of all cultic life in the period of the wilderness. That would contradict the witness of the Pentateuch and it appears rather unbelievable. He might be denouncing, not ritual in general, but those aspects of the cult that are of Canaanite origin, and be claiming implicitly those simpler but more authentic ceremonies. Verse 26 poses even more problems. Ought we to link it with v. 25 or with v. 27? In the former case it would be denouncing the idolatry to which Israel had succumbed so soon in the early days of its history, immediately after she was delivered from Egypt. In the second case, it would be announcing that Yahweh's people were about to fall into the power of foreign gods and to end their existence in exile (v. 27). Whatever the case may be, the Hebrew version we possess seems to have been corrected. The words *Sikkut* and *Kiyun* denote in all probability two Assyrian gods, *Sakkut* and *Kewan*, known elsewhere in connection with Saturn. The Greek text, on the other hand, supposes an original that is different from the Masoretic text, and this could be the more ancient. It might be reconstructed thus: 'Did you bring the tent (*sukkat*) of your king and the pedestal (*ken* or *kiyyon*) of your God . . .?' Amos would then be aiming not at idolatrous practices (the problem seems scarcely to have entered his mind) but at customs foreign to the cult of Yahweh that would witness to a deviation from the Israelite ritual. Whatever the precise sense of these verses may be, whose polemical nature we must not underestimate, Amos' general intention is clear since his utterance ends with an announcement about the deportation of the Israelites. In its turn then, this chapter ends with a tragic vision, for the exile actually signifies for Israel a kind of excommunication that is a form of death.

We should note that Amos 5:26 f was used by the Qumran community as is confirmed by a document called the 'Damascus Document'. On reading over the prophet Amos, the author of this document discovers God's purpose to save his own people by allowing them to live his Law in the 'land of Damascus'. That which is a threat of death for Amos' contemporaries thus becomes a pledge of survival for the members of the Essene community. The latter was established at Qumran, near the Dead Sea; moreover it came to be known symbolically as 'the land of Damascus'.

A curious fact is that one of the rare texts of Amos to be found in the New Testament is likewise Amos 5:25 ff; it appears at Acts 7:42 f. The author of Stephen's address is inspired by the Greek version, now somewhat modified. The mention of Damascus is replaced by that of Babylon with reference to the events of 587 B.C.

He sees in the prophet's declaration the proof that the Israelites' idolatry began during their stay in the Wilderness, and this agrees with his general viewpoint according to which the chosen people never ceased to resist their God and his witnesses.

The example of Qumran, like that which we find in Acts 7, shows us how and why Amos' words were reinterpreted by believing Jews and Christians in the period of the Roman Empire. They strove to find in the Scriptures a passage that would explain the present and determine the attitude of the faithful in the precise circumstances that they were experiencing. The interpretation that the New Testament has made of this passage does not prevent us, however, from returning to the words of Amos himself so as to let them challenge us directly in our turn.

Amos 6

This short chapter contains a number of elements. These can be divided up as vv. 1–7, 8–11, 12, 13–14. The RSV suggests however dividing the chapter as vv. 1–3, 4–7 (by adding at the beginning of v. 4 a 'woe' (*hoy*) as in v. 1) 8, 9–10 (in prose), 11–14. We find here Amos' familiar themes: (a) condemnation of an 'aristocracy' preoccupied above all else with enjoying life (vv. 1 ff); (b) announcement of the destruction of Samaria (vv. 8 ff); (c) denunciation of the wickedness inherent in the land (v. 12); and (d) a polemic against the illusions in which the Israelites persist in living (vv. 13–14). What strikes us here is the peculiar tone adopted by the prophet, his sarcastic irony and his slashing criticism of a populace that refuses to recognize the reality of the situation.

Chapter 6 commences with the funereal cry 'Woe . . .' (*hoy*). Following it is the picture of a city in ruins, piled high with corpses (vv. 8 ff); and it concludes with the threat of an invasion that will dumbfound the efforts at reconquering east Jordan, of which the government of Samaria is so proud (vv. 13 f). Once again Amos lets his hearers glimpse how the catastrophe is near and how death is prowling around the capital and its inhabitants. There is no escape from the living God and his wrath, when, in search for pleasure, security and comfort, one ignores the needs of others and makes a mock of justice. Such then is the warning with which Amos and the other prophets who follow him address us.

Amos 6:1–7   *Woe to the Choice Spirits Enjoying Themselves at their Ease*

In this 'imprecation' Amos turns against the political and other authorities who consider themselves to be sheltered within the walls of their city, and so, careless of the morrow, spend their time in festivity after festivity. He attacks their lack of conscience, their arrogance and their moral stance. This 'élite' is wallowing in luxury and sensuality without being in the least grieved at the world of misery known to their brethren (the '*ruin of Joseph*', v. 6b). In the prosperity of the time, life was sweet for some who stretched themselves upon beds of ivory, tasting tender meats, passing around cups of wine, and singing songs to the accompaniment of the harp!

The prophet brutally smashes the attraction of these banquets of the chosen few in society which go on long into the night, by a mournful *hoy*. He disturbs the fastidious and dubious atmosphere of these ceremonies where the other man's fate is completely disregarded. He upsets the revellers whose private means permit no refusal. After having portrayed the conduct of the leaders of the people (vv. 1–6) Amos utters a brief oracle of judgment (v. 7), introduced by the solemn formula: '*Therefore* ...'. We note the prophet's cruel irony: 'Those men who consider themselves the first (*reshit*) of the first', probably a reference to their election (v. 1b), will be the first (*rosh*) of those to go into exile. (v. 7a). There will be a 'finish' to their brawlings, and, according to some exegetes, to practices more or less blasphemous that had been inspired by a dubious religiosity.

It is astonishing to see the word *Zion* mentioned in 1, when the prophet's interest is virtually exclusively in the northern kingdom. Yet there is no justification for omitting this reference to the capital of Judah, as has been suggested. It is possible that Amos, aware of the links that existed between the courts of Judah and Israel, is aiming at a particular category of persons, at one social class, to be found in Jerusalem as well as in Samaria, and which calls for the same censuring of presumption and lack of conscience.

Verse 2 raises a difficulty. According to some commentators it might be making allusion to important cities of Syria and Philistia that met their end by submitting to the Assyrian armies between 738 and 711 B.C. If the text is Amos', that would imply that the prophet continued his activities in the south after his expulsion from Bethel and the death of king Jeroboam II, something that few historians will admit. Verse 2 must then be regarded as a note made by a disciple of the prophet, showing that Samaria would experience a fate comparable with that of the cities that were not able to resist the Assyrian invasion. Verse 2 would then be saying: 'You believe you can take refuge behind your fortifications; but look around you and see what has happened to cities just like yours. They gloried in their ramparts and defensive systems!'. But

v. 2 could have still another bearing. It is that the prophet was not expressing his own opinion, but was citing the arguments of the rulers of Jerusalem and Samaria as they congratulated themselves on the prosperity of their kingdoms, which was on a level with that of Calneh, Hamath or Gath. Verse 2 would then be witnessing to the inability of the Judean and Israelite authorities to realize the situation, as well as to their vanity. In consequence (v. 3), in believing that they could postpone the day of woe (the opposite of 5:18–20?), these authorities were actually establishing a reign (*shebet*) ('seat' in the RSV, 6:3) of violence.

Verses 4 ff describe the banquets that the notables rejoiced in: sumptuous furnishings, choice dishes, wine and music, in fact, nothing was lacking; but the contrast is striking and unbearable, in the light of Amos' final observation on '*the ruin of Joseph*' (v. 6b). The background to this invective, we discover once again, is the problem of justice. There are some who profit at the expense of the community; they enjoy life while the rest weep in misery. Amos does not desire a prosperity founded on oppression. That is why this fastidious set will be deported and this refined but rotten society will vanish away.

Amos 6:8–11   *Dead Bodies pile up in the Ruins of Samaria*

These verses, which are perhaps shaped out of various elements, picture for us the wrath of Yahweh upon Samaria and its consequent total liquidation. The passage is introduced by a solemn admonition from Yahweh, who declares that he hates Samaria and expresses his disgust at their strongholds. He has decided to rid himself of her altogether (v. 8). The God of Israel thus rejects the pretentious capital of the northern kingdom, and is about to deliver her up to punishment (an enemy invasion, an earthquake, an epidemic?).

Verse 9 specifies that those who survive the disaster will be stricken in their turn. The divine judgment spares no one at all (9:1 ff). Verse 10 then portrays the corpses that the divine scourge has left lying. The task devolves upon the nearest relative of the dead, *dor*, uncle on the paternal side, *mesareph*, uncle on the maternal side, according to J. L. Mays, or more generally, upon the one who incinerates the bodies; he has to concern himself with their remains, either cremating them (?) or just carrying their bones out of the house. The text is not very clear, so it may be reconstituted in various ways. But one fact is sure—there are many dead in the city where panic has seized the few still alive. These have the unenviable task of removing the corpses and of searching for possible survivors. Silence settles down at the moment when the wrath of Yahweh has struck and when there is the risk it might be unleashed again (v. 10). Verse 11 reveals that the God of Israel himself has ordered the destruction of all the homes in the city—does this point to an earthquake?—and has decided to reduce Samaria to a heap of ruins (Micah 3:12). It is on this declaration that this pericope concludes.

For Amos there exists a 'too late'. The time for delay is past. Israel is now under the stroke of the divine judgment. Every possibility of salvation is excluded. Nor does the Gospel permit us to take this message lightly.

Amos 6:12   *The Israelites' Senseless Attitude*

After the manner of a Wisdom teacher Amos invites his contemporaries to reflect on their conduct. He employs a simile, nay, a kind of parable (v. 12a) to enable the Israelites to discover for themselves the totally incomprehensible character of their behaviour (v. 12b). The prophet makes use of a rhetorical question to which the answer is obvious; clearly no one dreams of galloping horses over rocks nor of ploughing the seas with oxen (read *babaqar yam*). Yet Yahweh's people, when they falsify justice, are behaving in a manner that is simply ludicrous. We gather from this short utterance that the central theme of the case Amos is making against Israel is that the Israelites have turned the order of things upside down. The same verb (*haphak*) is employed to picture the fate of Sodom and Gomorrah (Gen. 19:21, 25, 29), where 'overthrow' really means 'turn upside down', that is, to destroy completely. In scorning the right, and in trampling on justice, Israel has acted in a deviant manner, has destroyed what lies at the basis of life, and has turned it into an instrument of corruption and ruin. Israel is to perish because in her heart justice has gone crazy.

We cannot be sure that the prophet's hearers understood the lesson. We can only wish it were so today, for, as the prophet reminds us, no one trifles with the right or with justice.

Amos 6:13–14   *A Small Victory that Hides a Great Disaster*

The Israelite armies have carried their successes to the east of Jordan. News of them reaches Samaria where there is great joy. The city honours its soldiers. Amos steps in with no regard for caution in order to ridicule those who cry 'Victory' and sows trouble in their minds. For him what is happening in the territory of Bashan is of no importance now that Israel will have to deal with a formidable enemy whom Yahweh himself is sending. The prophet's utterance begins perhaps with a *hoy* ('*Woe to you who rejoice . . .'* It comprises a kind of accusation (v. 13) followed by a threat introduced by *'For behold . . .'* (v. 14).

Verse 14 speaks of the nationalistic pride of the inhabitants of the northern kingdom. *Lo-debar* and *Karnaim* are both real localities situated in the area that Jeroboam II disputed with the Arameans and the Ammonites. Amos has chosen these two names with care, for the first, as the Versions have understood it, can mean 'for nothing', 'useless', and the second (lit. 'the two horns') is the pretext the Israelites seized upon to vaunt their own strength. In Amos' eyes the success at *Lo-debar* (Josh. 13:26 Hebrew; 2 Sam. 17:27) has no significance, and the victory at *Karnaim* is deceitful since it masks Israel's basic weakness.

The Israelites are about to measure themselves against an adversary, whom Amos does not name (Assyria?), but who is the instrument of the judgment that the God of Israel is pronouncing against his own people. The prophet is announcing to a people who occupy this territory reaching from the northern to the southern limits of the kingdom that the sum total of the work of Jeroboam II and of his father is of no account.

Chapter 6 ends then on the perspective of a political disaster rendering the 'couldn't care less' attitude of Samaria's leaders, indicated in his first couplets, all the more ridiculous and culpable. Woe awaits a nation whose authorities make proof of frivolity and blindness. They are dragging down the whole of Israel to its doom.

Part III

THE VISIONS OF AMOS AND HIS MESSAGE ABOUT THE END OF ISRAEL

Amos 7:1 to 9:10

In this last part, the prophet confirms his previous message and announces Israel's inevitable end. Essentially it comprises a series of visions to the number of five, the first four of which are basically alike. They can be grouped two by two, the last marking the prophet's final point in the establishment of his case. Today these are distributed throughout chapter 7 to 9 where they are accompanied by oracles whose severity is familiar to every reader of Amos' book. There is also a small biographical piece, the work of a disciple of the prophet, who describes the incident at Bethel, that is to say, the meeting between Amos and the supreme religious authority of the country, the priest Amaziah (7:10–17).

We might ask ourselves about the significance of the visions that Amos reports. Some have seen in them a kind of profession of faith as he recalls his spiritual journey and the source of his vocation. Others have thought that their purpose was to show how Amos had turned away from an official function in the service of the national God and of his people, in his capacity as 'the prophet of salvation', to a rather more charismatic and even revolutionary ministry, and how he had become a solitary and virulent witness against Israel, that is to say, a 'prophet of woe'. In reality the visions serve less to inform us of the prophet's states of mind than to reveal to us, by means other than his words, the meaning of Amos' intervention, in that they accompany his message, so as to clarify it and confirm it.

In general they are remarkably straightforward, and in this regard they differ from what is given us in the books of Zechariah and Daniel, and especially in Jewish apocalyptic. There we find bizarre scenes that need to be interpreted as they unfold before the eyes of the witnesses of the God of Israel. In fact in both Amos' and

Jeremiah's case (Jer. 1) they begin from <u>concrete and observable facts,</u> which under divine inspiration become bearers of a message and revealers of a truth that God is commmunicating to his spokesmen in order to enable them to accomplish their mission.

Amos 7:1–6   The First Two Visions, of the Locusts and of Fire

These two visions are constructed alike. They begin by recalling that the initiative behind each phenomenon goes back to Yahweh, who informs his witness about what is going to happen (v. 1 and v. 4). They tell us about the prophet's reaction even before he announces this double woe (v. 2 and v. 5), and inform us of the final divine decision (v. 3 and v. 6).

The first vision (vv. 1–3) has to do with a swarm of locusts that are devouring the winter grass (January–February). Their coming condemns the land to famine, for, after this date, the rains have almost ceased to fall and the grass no longer 'shoots up', 'after the king's mowings' (The king received the first crop of wheat); cf. 1 Kgs. 18:5. This only too frequent plague in the Near East is catastrophic for the local people (Exod. 10:12 ff; Deut. 28:38, 42; Joel 1). The second vision, in a pictorial manner, describes the dryness that menaces a region where the water sources are exhausted, as if by a fire that has struck at the stores of a subterranean sea, and which nothing is able to stop. This plague too endangers the very existence of all living beings in Israel. The future of God's people is on each occasion called in question.

In both instances Amos intervenes on Israel's behalf. He pleads the cause of the guilty party and succeeds in imploring God's pardon. Three matters deserve to be noted:

(a) Amos makes himself an intercessor, since his prophetic activity seems to demand it (Gen. 20:7; Jer. 15:1 ff; etc.). A revealing factor is that in spite of the harshness of his pronouncements with regard to the Israelites, Amos does not hesitate to appeal to the divine mercy.

(b) He makes a case of the smallness of Jacob, that is to say, of his frailty and vulnerability, and this at the precise moment when Israel thought herself to be great and strong. The arrogance of the ruling classes contrasts here with this humble, resolute and lucid prayer.

(c) Yahweh allows himself to be convinced by the pleading of his witness and 'repents' for striking the guilty party: the plague that has been announced will not come to pass. The issue of 'anthropopathism' in the Bible (the 'repentance' of Yahweh is the issue here) worries only those who conceive of God as an abstract, cold and distant idea. They have not understood how near the living God is to men and how he is able to share in their feelings.

Amos 7:7–8 and 8:1–3   *The Third and Fourth Visions, of 'Tin' and of Summer Fruit*

These two visions are constructed differently from the previous ones. The divine initiative (7:7; 8:1) is followed by a question put by Yahweh to which the prophet replies even before the God of Israel has concluded (quite different from what has preceded!; 7:8; 8:2).

The significance of the third vision (7:7–8) is subject to argument. It depends on the word *anak*, which is found only here in the O.T., though it occurs four times. Its meaning remains obscure. For some commentators *anak* means a plummet, and more particularly in this present case, a plumb-line that some unknown person—or Yahweh?—is holding in his hand and which is serving him as he measures to see if the wall of a building is upright. Yahweh, it seems, is 'measuring' Israel and is now passing judgment upon her (cf. 2 Kgs. 21:13). *Anak*, however, should rather be translated by 'tin', a metal used in the manufacture of armaments, and is thus a military symbol. By means of this vision Yahweh would thus be announcing the destruction of the city at the time of an invasion: *'Behold I am about to set "tin" in the midst of my people Israel'* (v. 8b). Some have suggested that the second *anak* should really be read as *anahah*, meaning 'sighing', 'moaning'. Playing with words, then, the prophet is saying that Yahweh is about to make his people lament, for he will cease to 'pass them by', that is to say, he will cease to spare them (Micah 7:18). Israel's fate is fixed, the people of Yahweh have allowed the respite to pass that God had been offering them, his condemnation is now imminent.

The sense of the fourth vision is clearer (8:1–3). Amos notices a basket of fruits at the end of summer (*qaits*). Questioned by Yahweh he says that the end (*qets*) has come upon the northern kingdom. Amos 8:2 is thus a decisive sentence, one that clarifies the whole of the prophet's message. Each one of Amos' interventions seems actually to evidence the fact that Israel is now lost, in that her God has decided to cease allowing her faults go unpunished. Verse 3 is probably an editorial addition that shows the effects of the divine wrath; the land is full of wailing, the corpses pile up, and silence reigns.

Amos 7:9–17   *The Incident at Bethel*

Verse 9 may also be an editorial addition meant possibly to

illustrate the consequences for Israel, in accordance with the third
vision (7:7–8), of the divine decision not to pardon his people.
Yahweh carries the attack right to the essential religious and
political basis on which the State of Israel depends. (Note the play
on words built from the root *h-r-b*.) It is possible on the other hand
that 9 was intended rather to introduce the narrative about the
meeting between Amaziah, who represented the clergy of Bethel,
and Amos, ending in the expulsion of the latter from the northern
kindgom (7:10 ff).

Verses 10–17 rest upon a direct witness; they comprise actually
three wordy confrontations. In the first one Amaziah denounces the
prophet to the king (vv. 10 f). In the second, he takes Amos to task
himself and orders him to leave the country as quickly as possible
(vv. 12 f). In the last, the prophet justifies himself by referring to
his vocation (vv. 14 f), and ends the dialogue by uttering a terrible
oracle against Amaziah that seems indirectly to involve also the
Israelites as a whole (vv. 16 f).

We should note the manner in which the individual responsible
for the cult at Bethel relates Amos' words to his king. He does not
quote the essential element in it, for he omits to point out that the
prophet is speaking in the name of Yahweh, the God of Jeroboam
II. It is significant that he allows it to be understood that Amos is
only a common political conspirator of whom the northern
kingdom had known more than one in its short history. The verb
qashar, to become bound to another, to conspire, recalls the only too
frequent coups d'état through which Israel had lived (1 Kgs. 15:27;
16:9; 2 Kgs. 9:14), and in which prophets had frequently been
involved (1 Kgs. 11:29 ff; 19:16; 2 Kgs. 2:3 ff). On his part
Amaziah, as his choice of words witnesses, desires above all else to
be the loyal servant of the royal power. He reminds Amos that he
has no right to speak within the sanctuary at Bethel since it belongs
directly to the court (v. 13). The high priest's attitude here is
debatable. In the eyes of some he shows only hostility and scorn
towards this southerner, this visionary, who has just emerged from
the countryside to occupy himself with affairs of state. Others
suppose that his attitude towards Amos must have been inspired
by worthy sentiments. Knowing the danger that this 'seer' was
courting, he could be suggesting that he should make himself
scarce, double quick! But above all, Amaziah seems to adopt the
position characteristic of the religious representative who does not
wish to have any trouble with the political authorities of the
country and so above all else wants to rid himself of a
trouble-maker. Among right thinking people, who find themselves
on a lofty social level, one would do anything to avoid having

problems. Thus it is that Amos is to be sacrificed for the peace of the kingdom.

Amos' reply is not lacking in dignity. He begins by maintaining his distance from the traditional prophets; these men wandered the country in groups, or attached themselves either to a court or to a sanctuary (1 Sam. 10:5, 6, 11). He had nothing in common with the official prophetic calling, which in the final analysis was at the service of any who would provide for them (v. 14). His present activity resulted solely from the divine initiative. He had been taken by Yahweh from his usual occupation, for he had an occupation that gave him a living, that of a 'herdsman' or a shepherd of sheep, perhaps as their owner, and whose food he prepared by cutting open sycamore fruits. Amos has nothing of 'a poor devil' about him, as has sometimes been believed, compelled to prophesy, such as those who told people's fortunes in order to make a living (Micah 3:5 ff). Yahweh himself had made him his spokesman to Israel his people (v. 15). Amos does not argue here about the principle of biblical prophecy, which already had a long history at the time of his appearance. Again some have claimed that he did do so. Rather he speaks with the marvellous and terrible freedom of one who knows himself to be the messenger of the God of Israel. Nothing then can restrain him, neither political nor religious powers, nor can anything divert him from his calling.

The prophet goes on to reveal to Amaziah the fate that awaits both him and his people—humiliation, exile, death. The chief fault in the high priest of Bethel is not, in Amos' eyes, that of having denounced him to the royal police, but his not having understood, or his having refused to see, that his intervention stemmed from the God whom Amaziah also claimed to serve. In dismissing Amos, then, Amaziah had betrayed his ministry; he was therefore to die in an unclean land where all contact with Yahweh would be forbidden him. It is possible that, in pronouncing this judgment beyond repeal, the prophet was thinking also of the fate awaiting the Israelites. They, like their high priest, called upon Yahweh, but did not listen to him who spoke in the name of the Lord.

This episode at Bethel remains a model of its kind. It describes the conflict between the power that is created when politics and religion make common cause and he who is the witness of the God of the Bible. History is full of encounters of this nature, when throne and altar combine to silence a person in one way or another, if he or she is imprudent enough to dare to proclaim to mankind the Word of God. For Christians the death of Christ is the most striking example of an attempt to silence one who spoke for God.

Amos 8

Over and above the fourth vision, which announces the disappearance of the northern kingdom (vv. 1 f), and the mournful scenes that this will occasion (v. 3), this short chapter contains a violent criticism of those merchants who are only interested in making money by any means available (vv. 4–8). It also contains a series of short utterances on the calamities that will strike Israel on that Day when her God will be her Judge (vv. 9–14). The prophet draws us step by step towards a time of desolation, of mourning and of death. No glimmer of light is going to pierce the dense night that will engulf Israel, the people of God.

Amos 8:4–8 *The Rapacity of her Tradesmen*

The favourable economic situation under Jeroboam II had provoked a frenzy of pleasure seeking and a desire always for more and more possessions. Commerce in agreement with the power of office exploited the weakest classes in the community; the city merchants monopolized trade by building up their stocks, thus allowing them to fix prices as they wished. Once again the 'poor' (vocabulary relating to poverty is employed not less than four times in this one prophetic utterance) are the victims of their brethren, contrary to the very clear demands of Yahweh. This time Amos summons the merchants, perhaps in Samaria's market place with a solemn '*Hear this word* . . .' (3:1; 4:1; 5:1). Not without indignation at their attitude he takes the side of the oppressed (vv. 5b ff), and concludes with a threat that implies a judgment: '*Surely I will never forget any of their deeds*' (v. 7).

We note that the prophet blames the guilty one for coveting (*shaaph*) or for trampling on (*shuph*, with the Versions) the poor (2:7), for seeking to ruin the poverty stricken (lit. put an end to them, annihilate them), or by manipulating them for their own ends, or again by buying them for money, for a derisory amount, probably by forcing them to pay their debts with the complicity of the judges. The land of Israel had become the place of 'trafficking in human beings', more precisely in peasants so deeply in debt that they were incapable of escaping from the clutches of pitiless moneylenders (v. 6).

In his usual way Amos quotes the statement of his adversaries (2:12; 4:1; 5:14; 6:2; etc.). Here the merchants complain at the frequency of new moons and sabbaths (v. 5a). At that period these were marked by celebrations at the sanctuaries with a consequent interruption of all commercial business dealings. It was only later on, particularly following upon the Exile, that the Sabbath came to be celebrated regularly on the seventh day of the week. It went on to assume a central place in the heart of Jewish tradition. In origin the Sabbath, which seems to have been coupled with the 'new moon', as in this passage, would possibly be a festival of the 'full moon'. Those days of 'stop-work' irritated the business circles who were in a hurry to sell their merchandize (v. 5a), Amos describes their behaviour, as they gave short supply, increased the size of their counter-weights, falsified their balances; in short, how they went in for organized theft. The first to suffer from such activities naturally were the impoverished folk. At the same time the business community 'served' them through getting rid of their cereal waste (vv. 5b f).

After this lengthy indictment Amos stops abruptly. The fact that Yahweh swears never to forget any of these proceedings, which their authors believed they were keeping secret, perhaps with the connivance of the authorities, results in a terrible threat hanging over them. Verse 8, which is taken up again in part at 9:5 within the framework of a hymn, may be secondary; but more probably the prophet resumes here, under the form of a question, with a cultic formula that the faithful repeat without noticing that they are singing about their own judgment. In face of all their crimes the land *'trembles'*, is heaved about, and its inhabitants plunged into mourning. The land falls and rises like the swelling of the Nile. Amos is once again in all probability referring to an earthquake. He is indicating particularly that it is just at that point where iniquity has its seat that world order is turned upside down. Injustice has cosmic consequences. Through their own fault people can imperil the harmony and even the existence of the earth. The consequences of scorning the 'poor', that is to say, of scorning the will of Yahweh go even as far as that, a fact that no one must ever forget!

Amos 8:9–10   Darkness and Bitterness

This short fragment, according to the solemn introduction to v. 9a, consists of an 'oracle of Yahweh'. In it we find likewise a formula: *'and on that day . . .'*, similar to that which occurs at 8:13; 9:11, as well as in the works of other prophets. Sometimes it takes on an eschatological nuance, as it points to events at the end of time (Isa. 27:1; Zech. 14:9; etc.). Compare also the expression: *'Behold, the days are coming . . .'* already to be found in Amos 4:2; 8:11; 9:13, but sometimes in secondary passages. According to the prophet it is Yahweh who is speaking and acting here; he it is who is sowing panic in the land, probably by causing an eclipse of the sun. In antiquity that was considered a fearful phenomenon, one that announced the end (Isa. 13:10; Joel 2:10; 2:30f; 3:15; etc.). We know of eclipses that took place in Palestine in 763 B.C. and even, according to H. W. Wolff, of a total eclipse of the sun on the seventh day of February, 784. Amos makes reference to what he has already said about the 'Day of the Lord' (5:18 ff; 8:9b), showing the terrible consequences of Yahweh's intervention, whereby the whole land is plunged into mourning of the cruellest type, that brought about by the death of an only son. All hope for life is definitely destroyed (Jer. 6:26; Zech. 12:10). The misery of this Day imprisons Israel in a despair from which nothing can bring her forth! Verse 10 recalls some of the rites observed on the occasion of the death of an Israelite—ritual weeping, sackcloth upon the loins, hair shaved off (5:16 f; Isa. 15:2 f; Micah 1:16; etc.). Once again (5:1 ff), with but a few strokes of the pen, the prophet describes the anguish that Israel is to experience on the day when Yahweh pronounces sentence upon her iniquity. Death thrusts itself upon Amos' spirit when he thinks of the future promised to the kingdom of Jeroboam II, for he keeps on endlessly turning back to it (5:1 ff, 16 f; 9:6, 8 ff; 7:17; etc.).

Amos 8:11–12   A Famine for the Word of Yahweh

This oracle, which opens in almost the same way as the preceding one, announces still another catastrophe; an extraordinary famine is to strike the whole land, not one brought about by an invasion of locusts or by a prolonged absence of rain (4:6 ff), but one that Yahweh himself brings about by remaining silent. When they had had the chance, his people had not wanted to listen to the prophet. They had chased him from their territory. So now they find themselves facing the silence of their God. All communication between God and his own people is broken (v. 11). Now, Israel cannot live without the Word of Yahweh (Deut. 8:3; Matt. 4:3 f). She is thus condemned to wander from one corner of the land to the other—the expression *'from sea to sea'* describes symbolically the two extremes of the region (Ps. 72:8; Zech. 9:10)—but in vain. Yahweh has shut himself up in his silence and in this way manifests his condemnation of a guilty nation. The Israelites are running foul of the 'No' that their God utters in the absence of all dialogue with them, in fact, they are excommunicated. For God too there exists 'a time to keep silence, and a time to speak' (Eccles. 3:7). It is a question of being prepared to listen when the God of the Bible addresses his Word to us.

Amos 8:13–14   The 'Vital Forces' of the Nation are to Fall, Victims of Idolatry

This last declaration in chapter 8 is connected with what precedes by the linking word 'thirst' (vv. 11 and 13). It could be in part the work of a disciple; v. 14a would then, for some commentators, be secondary. If so it should be read either after 8:9 f, or following upon 5:1 f. Various interpreters suggest it contains two elements that are now placed together:

(a) the announcement of the definitive disappearance of the young girls and the young men, who represent Israel's future, her 'vital forces': *'They shall faint . . . they shall fall, and never rise again'* (vv. 13, 14b). These ought to have assured her of a glorious existence in the days to come. In a word, it is now all over with the people of Yahweh, stricken beyond all possibility of renewal. On the horizon of this oracle there is outlined once again the death of the northern kingdom.

(b) In the present version of the passage, the blame lies upon those young people who reveal a dubious, syncretistic attitude, in the way in which they associate the worship of Yahweh with idolatrous practices that are probably of Canaanite origin. There are minor divinities named here, such as *ashmat*, the 'sin' of Samaria. (Perhaps we should read 'the' *Asherat*, a kind of divine symbol.) Or else 'the' *ashmat*, from the name of a Syrian goddess (2 Kgs. 17:30), or we should read 'divinities' such as are mentioned in 1 Kgs. 12:30, calves of gold worshipped at *Dan*, and in Amos 5:5, where we learn that worship occurs at *Beer-sheba*. These shrines were to be found at the northern and the southern extremities of the country (Jud. 20:1; 1 Sam. 3:20; 2 Sam. 17:11, etc.). People have sometimes corrected the word *derek*—meaning, with the RSV, 'way', 'road', and by extension, 'pilgrimage'—into *dod*, that is, 'beloved'. For this title could apply equally to a god (as here in the RSV). But none of these will be of any use in the Day of the Lord. The local gods, 'forces', on whom the people and even the youth had tended to rely instead of putting their whole confidence in their God, would save no one at the hour of judgment. Yahweh refuses to share with any other (Exod. 20:3; Matt. 6:24). Because they had forgotten that, the northern kingdom would collapse, never to rise again (v. 14b).

Amos 9

This last chapter is made up of a number of pieces, the first of which deals with the end of the northern State. These are mostly Amos' own work; the last, beginning at v. 11, or perhaps v. 8, constitutes a later addition for which the prophet does not seem to be responsible. We shall handle vv. 11–15 separately. They form a kind of epilogue to Amos' book.

We meet successively in vv. 1–10 with the issues that are

handled in the first part: (a) a brief mention of the fifth vision allowing Amos to announce the extermination of the guilty nation (vv. 1–4); (b) a fragment of a hymn that recalls parallel passages (4:13; 5:8 f); (c) a declaration by the prophet assigning Israel her true place amongst the nations (9:7); (d) a new threat, perhaps corrected and completed later on against the sinful kingdom (vv. 8–10). All these documents taken together confirm that the end has come for the Israelites, as Amos had proclaimed right from his first utterances.

Amos 9:1–4   *The Fifth Vision and what it Implies*

The fifth vision is clearly different from those that precede it (7:1 ff; 8:1 f); it is just sketched in the Hebrew text and is immediately followed by a divine Speech (v. 1a). Yahweh himself is its object, and it is he who commands the destruction of a sanctuary, most probably that of Bethel, the most important in the northern kingdom. The dialogue between God and his prophet is here replaced by a command addressed to someone who is not expressly named—it would seem to be a member of the heavenly court rather than Amos himself. The command is to smite the capitals of the temple in such a manner that the very thresholds themselves would shake and that the entire building would crash down on the worshippers assembled there. The text, as we have it, is often altered by commentators removing some words and correcting some verbal forms resulting in a version that could be the original and which offers the advantage of clarity. The revised text reads: 'I saw the Lord high above the altar; he struck the capitals and the thresholds shook. And he says, "I will shatter them . . ."' (v. 1a). Thus reconstructed the scene is not unlike the inaugural vision of Isaiah's ministry (Isa. 6:1 ff).

Yahweh's presence over the altar is normally a pledge of safety for his own people. In the present case it is just the contrary, since the divine announcement is explicit: what Yahweh intends is nothing less than the total annihilation of the sinful Israelites (vv. 1b–4a). There will be no possibility of escaping the justice of Yahweh. All possible hypotheses are considered only to be successively discarded. Those who might escape the initial catastrophe, probably an earthquake, (*ra'ash*), will fall with the sword from which not one of them shall escape (v. 1b). even if the Israelites in their panic, and using the most desperate means, should attempt not to fall into the hands of God, God is able to catch up with them to punish them. He will find them even if they have taken refuge in the underworld, *Sheol*, where nevertheless Yahweh intervenes so rarely that he seems to have no contact with the dead (Ps. 6:5; 88:5; etc.; conversely at Prov. 15:11; Job 26:6; etc.). Neither heaven (v. 2), nor the abundant vegetation on the top of Carmel will serve as an adequate hiding place from God. The bottom of the sea seems to be so far removed from Yahweh that it might appear to offer a sure refuge; but, Yahweh says: '*There I will command the Serpent*', a sort of marine monster, *and it shall bite them*' (v. 3); Finally, the hope that in exile, beyond the land of Israel, it should be easier to escape from their God was in vain (v. 4a). There is something grandiose and terrible about this relentlessness of Yahweh in pursuing his own people in order to judge them: '*My hand shall take them . . . I will bring them down . . . I will search out . . . I will command . . .*' concluding with a kind of curse, '*I will set my eyes upon them for evil and not for good*' (v. 4b). Yahweh's look, which is the source of salvation and of peace, becomes here the cause of anguish and of death. Such then is the comment that Amos adds to his fleeting yet eloquent vision that he has had on the future of the temple at Bethel.

This passage cannot help but remind us of the Wisdom tradition, and particularly of Ps. 139. This psalm expresses the faith of a believer who knows it is not possible to escape from one's God (vv. 7–12). Yet what a contrast there is between the confession of the psalmist with his serene wonder at the wisdom and omnipresent power of his God and this declaration by our 8th century prophet who places no bounds upon Yahweh's wrath and leaves his people no hope at all! In this way, then, the cycle of visions closes. If, as S. Amsler suggests, the first two revealed Yahweh's *patience* with a sinful nation, and the two following 'the *irrevocable* nature of his decision to be done with Israel', then the last 'illustrates the *unavoidable* nature of the condemnation that towers over the Israelites': Yahweh has the power to make appeal not only to history or to nature, but also to the whole cosmos (the sky, the sea, and even to *sheol*) to exercise his judgment against the Israel of the north. No one at all, no matter where he may seek refuge, even in the hereafter, will escape the God of the Fathers, the God of Amos, and the God of Jesus Christ!

Amos 9:5–6   *Fragment of a Hymn*

Before the unleashing of the divine wrath Amos, or more probably an editor of his book, thought that there remained only to give glory to Israel's God. He has inserted here also (4:13; 5:8 f) a portion of a hymn that celebrates Yahweh and his power that is both creative and destructive at once. These verses recall other quotations from hymns (9:5 and 8:6; 9:6b and 5:8b) that lay stress on the control over the entire cosmos by Israel's God. But the manner in which this is described here has a threatening character, which is inescapable when one hears or reads the preceding verses. Yahweh is in fact represented to us particularly as he who, if he but touches the earth, causes it to tremble, and who instigates mourning amongst its inhabitants; or again, as he who causes it to stand or fall according to his pleasure—is there here also a reference to an earthquake?—or even as he who, from on high in his abode, pours out the waters upon the earth like the Deluge, in order to annihilate his creation. Not only are Israel's days numbered (vv. 1–4) but the earth itself is in danger owing to the wickedness of the people of Yahweh.

Amos 9:7   A Dispute about Israel's Status

This sentence, in the eyes of some commentators, would mark the end of the basic collection of Amos' utterances, what follows being the work of his disciples in the course of time. It forms an example of the literary genre known as 'controversy', and, like 3:1 f, places the prophet over against his opponents. In face of Amos' threatening speeches, which call the whole future of Yahweh's people in question, his hearers retort by appealing to Israel's election (3:1 f), or, as in this instance, to the initial fact of 'salvation history'. To it the Tradition keeps on returning, to the Exodus, to the Flight from Egypt, that marvellous act of liberation on which the existence of the Israelites was founded and which guaranteed their future destiny. The Exodus had, in a way, created Israel. To it she owed everything and thanks to it she could go forward, confident of the days to come.

In this polemical series of questions Amos combats, not the fact of the 'ascent from Egypt', but the consequences that his contemporaries draw from it. Once again he is in complete disagreement with them when he dares to compare what Yahweh has done for his own people with the fate of the Philistines and the Syrians, those two powerful enemies of Israel. Israel had had to suffer so much in the wars she had waged against them. Amos has the impudence to say that the God of Israel had brought them up (them!) from their place of origin! In the case of the Philistines this was *Caphtor*, indentified by most with Crete, but sometimes also with Cappodocia or some other region in Asia Minor. In the case of the Syrians, this was probably *Kir* in Mesopotamia or possibly *Ur*. But no one knows today for certain. For Amos, the important thing is not the fixing of the point of departure, the place from which these nations were displaced, but to show that their itinerary was dependent upon the same Providence as the One who had been concerned with Israel's ancestors, held as slaves in Egypt, and

who had permitted them to regain their freedom and finally to
obtain a home in the land of Canaan.

Amos even has the audacity to compare the Israelites to the
Ethiopians, the people who dwelt in the region of the Upper Nile,
in Abyssinia or in Nubia. They appeared to the Israelites at that
period to be a people afar off, and consequently afar off from
Israel's God. There is here not a single note either of depreciation
or of racism in the prophet's words, simply a statement that would
appear extraordinary and even unacceptable to his hearers, that
their God was equally interested in those strange far away peoples
who lived to the south of Egypt. Amos is not doing away with the
privileges of Yahweh's people, as once was thought, he is just
reminding the Israelites that their God remains Master of his
choices, and that his solicitude is not limited to Israel. He opposes
the pretensions of the people of the northern kingdom in their
monopolizing of Yahweh's benevolent activities and in making use
of his interventions when he acts in their favour, yet disobeying his
commandments and treating his will with contempt. This short
verse opens up universalistic perspectives that are not foreign to the
message of the Old Testament, but which are only too often
neglected. The election of Israel does not imply that Yahweh is
uninterested in the other nations; in fact, on the contrary, he set
free Israel first (the Exodus) in order to guarantee the liberation of
the whole of humanity (Gen. 12:1 ff).

Amos 9:8-10   Sinners Alone will be Smitten

These verses raise some difficulties. Verse 8 might be understood to
be the continuation of vv. 1-4 (as the RSV), or as the conclusion to
what had immediately preceded it (v. 7). If the latter, then Yahweh
condemns every sinful kingdom, whichever it may be; Amos would
be announcing that Israel is to be destroyed, just as has already
happened to the Amorites (*shamad*, 2:9). But v. 8 contradicts the
prophet's declarations, notably at the beginning of this chapter. So
this must be the work of a Judean who distinguishes between the
sinful nation (Israel) and Judah, which had survived the judgment
up till now, The idea that Yahweh is going to sort out his own
people, finding expression in vv. 9 f, is not attested elsewhere in
Amos' message. It could be equally relegated to a later
commentator who was seeking to accommodate the prophetic word
to the realities of his time. That is, by 721 not all the people of
Yahweh had been wiped out, since Judah was still in existence; and
this was so even beyond 587, in that an exilic community continued
to survive the disaster. The editor therefore spoke of the divine
judgment in the perspective, opened by the interventions of

Jeremiah and Ezekiel. Both of these had insisted on the fact that the God of Israel knew how to distinguish between the righteous and sinners (Jer. 31:29 f; Ezek. 18:1 ff).

In fact, Yahweh is not going to punish the faithful with the ungodly. The image of the 'sieve', borrowed from agricultural life, is witness of this. He is going to shake Israel in order to separate the good grain from the 'pebbles': these will be retained by the strainer (v. 9). They represent the sinners, conscienceless and arrogant, destined for the sword (v. 10). Another way of reading it, one that would again be later than Amos since it presupposes the exile, along with the mention of *'among all the nations'*, is that Yahweh would be assembling those Jews in the diaspora who had remained attached to him (defined here by the word 'pebble') in order to save them (v. 9). He would then be destining all the guilty to death (v. 10). We can see how Amos' successors have understood and reinterpreted his message in the light of the new events that Israel had lived through since the 8th century.

This chapter, which begins with the most radical of condemnations (*'Not one of them shall escape'*, vv. 1 ff), is followed by an updating of those responsible for this book of prophecy (only *'all the sinners shall die . . . who say, "Evil shall not overtake or meet us"'* (v. 10), before concluding by still more positive views (11 ff). It witnesses to the importance of the statement that each member of the people of Yahweh is responsible for his own fate (Ezek. 18), an affirmation whose role will increase both during and after the exile, yet not without posing grave problems for the Jewish faith, as the book of Job attests.

EPILOGUE

Amos 9:11–15   The Time of Salvation

Two oracles comprise the conclusion to Amos' book. Each of them announces a new era of prosperity for Yahweh's people. The first speaks of the restoration of the Davidic kingdom (vv. 11 f), and the second, the fullness of the time of salvation (vv. 13 ff). Opinions about attributing these verses to Amos are very divided, and the discussion continues even today. Meanwhile it appears that there exist strong arguments for maintaining that these passages do not date from the 8th century, but from the exile or from the period following it. They would then be the work of a distant disciple of Amos who, under the inspiration of the Spirit, will have added this consolatory ending to the prophet's gloomy message.

Reasons of a literary, historical and doctrinal nature unite in fact to make us adopt this point of view. The vocabulary and the expressions that one reads here, like 'the days of old', or the formula *'shubh shebuth'* ('restore the fortunes') belong principally to the post-exilic prophetic literature (Isa. 63:9; Micah. 7:14; Jer. 29:14; Joel 3:18; etc.); the mention of *'the booth of David that is fallen'* (9:11), with its breaches and its ruins, does not fit with the situation of Amos' day, but with the period near the exile, or the exilic period itself (587–538). And so with the expression *'the remnant of Edom'*, which seems to imply the fate of the Edomites when they were occupied by the Babylonians in the 6th century B.C. (Ezek. 25:12 ff; 35:1 ff). The marvellous future promised here (9:13 ff) contrasts with what Amos had said about the Day of the Lord (5:18 ff), and especially it does not correspond at all with what appears as the dominant theme of the prophet's preaching, namely, justice. One would expect Amos to announce the judgment still to come, one in which a reign of justice would be instituted that would permit the whole people to flourish. In a word, everything seems to indicate that here we are in the presence of one or of several additions to the prophet's utterances.

Certainly it is possible that Amos could also have made a speech of encouragement for his questioners, but we have no knowledge of any, and if he had made such an assertion he would probably have expressed himself differently. This conclusion is important when it is a question of reconstituting Amos' message with the greatest possible exactitude, and it confirms that it was one of extraordinary severity for the Israelites to the north. He had left them with practically no hope of escaping the wrath of their God, and goes on to fully justify this attitude. In this regard Amos' position remains of a pattern; he shows us that it is not possible to render worship to the God of the biblical Revelation while trifling either openly or secretly with man made in the image of God. Once again 'the summary of the Law' recapitulates perfectly the thought of the prophet.

But the author of the oracles that conclude the book of Amos had a sound intuition, and it is important to underline this. In accordance with his tradition he has indicated that the divine plan for Israel could not end solely with its disappearance in the course of frightful scenes of wars, epidemics, cataclysms. Judgment was not Yahweh's last word upon his own people. Between God and his people a new page had to be written in a totally different manner, and based solely upon divine grace.

Amos thus remains the witness to the 'No' that God says to the guilty nation, but his anonymous commentator adds a 'nevertheless' whose profound reality is demonstrated for Christians by the Cross and the Resurrection.

The first oracle (vv. 11 f) brings forward the political aspect of the renewal of the people of Yahweh. Starting from the lamentable situation in which the '*booth of David*' finds itself—the expression points to the kingdom of David rather than to his dynasty! This fits probably with the period that has either preceded or followed the southern State's last moments. Yahweh promises to intervene and reconstruct her '*as in the days of old*'. We should note the importance of the verbs employed here with Yahweh as subject. The author is perhaps referring back to the Davidic tradition attested particularly in 2 Sam. 7:11 ff, 27 ff. Verse 12 envisages a kind of reconstituted Davidic empire; it refers also the Edomites—'*the remnant of Edom*'—as if they had undergone the Babylonian occupation, now being amongst the first to be placed under the control of Judah. But the recovery of those territories that were formerly subject to King David and which, in general, had been placed under Yahweh's jurisdiction, was not to stop there (Amos 1–2).

The second oracle (vv. 13–15) seeks to express the abundance (*shalom*) that will characterize the new age established by Yahweh. Possibly it is not from the same hand as that of the preceding oracle. This text pictures the acceleration of agricultural tasks resulting from the participation of nature in this era of prosperity. The soil, now prodigiously fertile, will permit the succession, without the one overtaking the other, of the work of the farm-labourer, of the reaper, of the vintager, and of the sower. The mountains shall drip sweet wine (v. 13; Joel 3:18), work shall no longer be a curse (Gen. 3:19), and the land of Israel shall have become once again 'a land flowing with milk and honey' (Exod. 3:8; Deut. 11:9; Ezek. 20:6; etc.).

Verses 14 f indicate the radical transformation that the people of Yahweh ('*my people Israel*') will experience. The expression '*shub shebut*' covers not only the return from exile, something that had long been proclaimed, but also a complete change in the destiny of a nation, or of the world. Israel is thus re-established in her land (lit. '*I will plant them . . . and they shall never again be plucked up*'; v. 15; Jer. 24:6; 31:8; Isa. 60:21), and they shall enjoy to the full the fruit of their labours. The Israelites are to rebuild the ruined cities and inhabit them, plant vineyards and drink their wine, cultivate gardens and eat their produce (v. 14). This effective power of human labour is a sign of the divine blessing (Deut. 28:1 ff; Lev. 26:3 ff; as against Deut. 28:15 ff; Lev. 26:14 ff; Amos 5:11); it plays a part also in the 'eschatological' prosperity (Isa. 61:4; 62:8; 65:21 ff). It is on this idyllic vision that the book of Amos concludes. We would be wrong, in the name of some kind of spiritual view of life, not to take such perspectives seriously, for they remind us that the God of Israel concerns himself with concrete and not imaginary beings, with real and not with fictitious problems that people like us meet with here below. The hope which inspires the Old Testament and of which Amos and his followers each in his own way becomes the echo, is taken up in a declaration of the New Testament: 'We wait for new heavens and *a new earth, in which righteousness dwells*' (2 Peter 3:13).

We should note that Amos 9:11 is attested in the Qumran texts, in a selection of passages such as 2 Sam. 7:10–14 and fragments of Psalms 1 and 2, which have a messianic connotation. The prophet of the 8th century was read within the Essene context as a witness to the coming of the Messiah who was to save Israel (4 Qflor 10 ff). It is Amos 9:11 f. that is cited again in the N.T. by the author of the book of Acts. He makes use of the Greek version of the O.T., which differs from the Hebrew, at Acts 15:15 ff. According to the interpretation that James gives us in his discourse Amos would have been announcing not only the raising up of 'the booth of David', that is to say, the Messiah, but he would be referring also to the conversion of the nations to Christ. Actually, according to him, 'the rest of man' (*adam*, in place of *edom*) will seek (*yidreshu*, in place of *yirshu*) the Lord. In conferring a universalistic perspective on the prophet's declaration James permits the apostles to resolve the prickly problem of the status of Christians of pagan origin in the bosom of the Church (Acts 15:19 ff). The prophet, announcer of the end of Israel, thus becomes witness to the unity of believers of every lineage in the worship of the only God and of his Christ.

BIBLIOGRAPHY

Commentaries

S. Amsler. *Commentaire de l'Ancien Testament XIa: Amos* (Neuchâtel-Genève, 1965, 1982²).

J. P. Hyatt. *Peake's Commentary on the Bible: Amos* (Edinburgh, 1962).

H. McKeating. *The Cambridge Bible Commentary: The Books of Amos, Hosea and Micah* (New York, 1971).

J. L. Mays. *Old Testament Library: Amos, a Commentary* (London, 1969).

W. Rudolph. *Kommentar zum Alten Testament: Amos,* (Gütersloh, 1971).

H. W. Wolff. *Biblischer Kommentar Altes Testament: Amos,* in *Dodekapropheten 2* (Neukirchen-Vluyn, 1969, 1975²) = Hermeneia (Philadelphia, 1977).

Various Studies

J. Barton, *Amos' Oracles against the Nations: A Study of Amos* 1:3–2:5 (Society for Old Testament Study, Monograph Series 6, Cambridge 1980).

F. Horst, *Die Doxologien im Amosbuch,* Zeitschrift für die alttestamentliche Wissenschaft 47, (Giessen-Berlin, 1929), 45–54. (= *Gottes Recht, Studien zum Recht im Alten Testament,* Theologische Bücherei 12. (München, 1961), 155–166.

A. S. Kapelrud. *Central Ideas in Amos* (Oslo, 1956, 1961²).

H. Martin-Achard. *Amos, L'homme, le message, l'influence* (Geneva, 1984).

A. Neher. *Amos: Contribution à l'étude du prophétisme* (Paris, 1950, 1981²).

G. von Rad, *Old Testament Theology,* Vol. 1: *The Theology of Israel's Historical Traditions* (Edinburgh, London, New York 1962) Vol. 2: *The Theology of Prophetic Traditions* (1965).

H. Graf Reventlow. *Das Amt des Propheten bei Amos: Forschungen zur*

Religion und Literatur des Alten und Neuen Testaments 8e (Göttingen, 1962).

J. de Waard, *The Chiastic Structure of Amos* V. *1–17.* (Vetus Testamentum 27), (Leiden, 1977), 170–177.

H. W. Wolff. *Amos' geistige Heimat; Wissenschaftliche Monographien zum Alten and Neuen Testament 18* (Neukirche-Vluyn, 1964) = *Amos the Prophet,* (Philadelphia, 1973).

THE THEOLOGY OF HOPE

A Commentary on the Book of

Lamentations

S. PAUL RE'EMI

I wish to put on record my gratitude both to the Rev. Professor Robert Davidson, of Glasgow, and to the Very Rev. Professor George Knight, of Auckland, for their sustained help as I strove to give this Commentary its final form.

S. Paul Re'emi

CONTENTS

INTRODUCTION

The Meaning and Purpose of Lamentations

The Book of Lamentations contains five songs, one in each of the book's five chapters. In these songs the author meditates on the tragedy of the fall of the kingdom of Judah and especially on the destruction of the Temple, which was so sacred to the people of Israel. The fall of Jerusalem is described in 2 Kgs. 25:1–12, as well as in Jer. 52:3b–16. The siege of Jerusalem by the armies of Babylon came as a consequence of the rebellion of Zedekiah, king of Judah, against the king of Babylon (2 Kgs. 24:20b). 'So the city was besieged till the eleventh year of King Zedekiah (587 B.C.). On the ninth day of the fourth month the famine was so severe in the city that there was no food for the people of the land. Then a breach was made in the city; the king with all the men of war fled by night by the way of the gate between the two walls, by the king's garden . . .' (2 Kgs. 25:2–4). King Zedekiah went with them. The Babylonian army overtook him in the plains of Jericho, and he was captured. His soldiers were taken prisoner or fled, and Zedekiah was taken to the king of Babylon at Riblah, where sentence was pronounced against him. Zedekiah's sons were killed before his eyes; then they put out Zedekiah's eyes, bound him with chains, and took him to Babylon.

'In the fifth month, on the seventh day of the month—which was the nineteenth year of King Nebuchadnezzar, king of Babylon—Nebuzaradan, the captain of the bodyguard, a servant of the king of Babylon, came to Jerusalem. And he burned the house of the Lord, and the king's house and all the houses of Jerusalem; every great house he burned down . . . And the rest of the people who were left in the city . . . Nebuzaradan carried into exile . . . But the captain of the guard left some of the poorest of the land to be vinedressers and ploughmen' (2 Kgs. 25:8–12).

All but the last poem seem to have been written either during the siege of the city or immediately after the collapse of all resistance. The behaviour of the occupying troops towards the crestfallen remnant of the population seems to have been as cruel and bitter as anything they had had to experience during the siege. By this time, moreover, the elite of the people had evidently been deported by the Babylonians to exile some 700 miles away. Those whom we meet now in Lamentations seem to be 'the poorest of the land', those whom the captain of the guard had allowed to remain.

Lamentations served the survivors of the catastrophe in the first place as a means of expressing their grief and horror. The best way for men to live through the grief and shock of a calamity is by facing it, by measuring its dimensions, by finding words to order and to express their feelings. And secondly, it reminded them of their past glory, which brought a gleam of light into their darkness and humiliation.

Yet this book is not only an expression of grief and sorrow, it is also a confession of sin. It witnesses to the truth of the utterances of such prophets as Amos, who had lived some 170 years earlier than the fall of Jerusalem in 587 B.C. The people had been misled by iniquitous leaders. Yet in this the whole nation was responsible before God for their disloyalty to the Covenant, so that the blame could not be lightly passed on to false prophets and complacent priests. These had cried 'Peace, peace' when there was no peace (Jer. 6:14; 8:11). But individuals were just as much responsible for the 'end' that had come upon Jerusalem, in that they had followed the crowd without discernment. The poet acknowledges in the name of the people that this calamity that had fallen upon Judah was in fact a punishment from Yahweh. It was the Day of the wrath of God of which Amos had spoken. But at the same time, therefore, it was a warning for the generations to come, not only for Judah, but for all the nations of the world as well.

The poet recognizes, as none before him had done so completely, that God waits until his disloyal people are at last aware that of themselves they are nothing, and that they cannot rescue themselves from the pit into which they have sunk. Yet God's purpose and plan for the world through them will continue—but by grace alone.

Thus it is, that in the midst of the gloom and darkness, in the midst of this desperate calamity that has overtaken Yahweh's people, living as they are now under the brutality of their cruel conquerors, there appears a gleam of light. One individual, and only one, it seems, arises with a call of hope, of hope in the mercies of God. And so he appeals to his brethren to examine their ways and return to the Lord with all their heart. Though Israel may fail God, God will not forsake Israel for ever (Lam. 3:22, 31).

1. The Name of the Book

The name 'Lamentations' comes from the Septuagint, the Greek version of the Old Testament. There it is entitled 'Threnoi', while in the Vulgate, the Latin version, it is 'Threni'. In the Hebrew tradition it is known as 'Qinot', which name we find also in the Talmud (*Baba Batra* 15a). Yet in the Hebrew Bible it has the name '*Eika*' i.e. 'How?'—from the first word of the book in Hebrew.

Hebrew tradition ascribes the authorship of the book to Jeremiah, as does the Talmud (*Baba Batra* 15a) and the Targum (the Aramaic version of the Old Testament). Likewise the Septuagint introduces the book with the following words: 'After Israel was carried into captivity and Jerusalem was laid waste, Jeremiah sat down and wept, and sang this song of woe over Jerusalem'. In most of the Versions the book of 'Lamentations' is placed after the book of Jeremiah as a kind of epilogue. This tradition is based on 2 Chr. 35:25, where it is written: 'Jeremiah also uttered a lament for Josiah; and all the singing men and singing women have spoken of Josiah in their laments to this day. They made these an ordinance in Israel; behold, they are written in the Laments.' The name '*Qinah*' is used in Hebrew for any lament (dirge) such as was uttered by prophets, poets or kings; for example, there is the lament on the deaths of King Saul and of his son Jonathan spoken by David (2 Sam. 1:17); there are laments by Jeremiah (Jer. 7:29; 9:10; 9:19), by Ezekiel (Ezek. 19:1; 26:17; 27:2, etc.) and by Amos (Amos 5:1). These laments were special songs composed in mourning for the dead, or on the occasion of a great national catastrophe. There were special singers (mostly women) hired for these occasions. We read of these in 2 Chr. 35:25, and in Jer. 9:17. Even to this day such singers are employed in the East for weeping and mourning for the dead, especially in Arab countries, by Muslims and Christians alike. There is no doubt that the songs of 'Lamentations' belong to this class of literature. But they contain other elements as well, such as confession of sin and expressions of penitence and hope. Moreover, as we shall see later, they also show acquaintance with the Wisdom literature.

2. Its Place in the Canon

The canonicity of the book of 'Lamentations' was never disputed. Yet, while in the Septuagint it is placed after the book of Jeremiah—and so too in the Latin version to be followed by other languages—in the Hebrew it was placed right from the beginning in the third part of the Old Testament. This was known as 'the

Writings' (in Hebrew: *Ketubim*), or '*Hagiographa*' in Greek and Latin. Yet, even so, its place in the Hebrew canon, in the book of 'Writings', was not altogether fixed. The Massoretes, the Jewish scholars who edited the text of the Old Testament in the 7th–8th centuries A.D., made it one of the 'Five Scrolls', or *Megilloth*, each of which had come by this time to be read at one of the great Jewish festivals. Lamentations formed part of the liturgy for the day on which the Fall of Jerusalem was commemorated, viz., the 9th day of Ab (June–July). We can see how the last of our Songs, chapter 5, was used in this way right from the beginning.

3. FORM AND TYPES

The book of Lamentations contains five separate songs, each song forming a chapter. The first four songs are acrostics, i.e. the strophes open with successive letters in the Hebrew alphabet. This form of poetry was considered in its time a special work of art. It is also found in later poems of the Old Testament, for example in Psalms (25; 34; 37; 111; 112; 119; 145) and in Proverbs (31:10–31). In the first song the Hebrew letters are in the usual order but in chapters 2 and 4 the letter 'Pe' comes before the 'Ayin', instead of 'Ayin' before 'Pe'. Some commentators suppose that the reason for this irregular order is that when these songs were compiled the order of the alphabet had not yet been finally fixed.

These songs deserve the name of 'laments' if we judge them according to their form and content. However, some commentators would designate the fifth song as a 'prayer' rather than as a 'lament'. The rhythm of each strophe is characteristic of the Hebrew lament, where each verse is divided into two parts, the first being longer and the second shorter; the proportion is usually 3:2 or 4:3. A classic example of this rhythm is found in song 3, which is also the best from a purely literary point of view. In the first two laments the strophes have three double verses each; each strophe beginning with a Hebrew letter in alphabetical order. The third song likewise contains three double verses, but each verse in the strophe begins with the same letter in alphabetical order. This reminds us of Psalm 119, which contains strophes of eight verses, where all eight begin with the same Hebrew letter. The fourth song contains strophes of two verses each; the first verse of each strophe beginning with a Hebrew letter, again in alphabetical order. The fifth song is not an acrostic, but is composed of twenty two verses, the number of letters in the Hebrew alphabet.

The book of Lamentations can be considered as a literary creation of the first rank. 'Of the fourteen acrostics in the Old

Testament the book of Lamentations stands alongside Psalm 119 as the largest in scope and execution. It is incomparably the finest in its careful detail and subtlety of development ... Like a great cathedral, its unity is broken in innumerable pleasing ways, never distracting but always contributing to the total impression' (N. K. Gottwald: *Studies in the Book of Lamentations*, p. 23). Just as the form of the songs is that of mourning, so also are their contents. Chapters 1, 2 and 4 are written in the rhythm used for dirges (songs for the dead). Yet we can distinguish different elements in the contents of these songs; there are national laments (2:22; 3:43–47; and ch. 5), and individual laments (1:9c–11c, 12–16). There are also complaints and thanksgiving songs (3:1–24, 52–66), a wisdom song (3:25–27), confession of sins (1:5, 8, 14, 18, 20; 3:39–42; 4:6), and hymns (3:22 ff; 5:19). This connection between different elements or different types of songs—mourning, wisdom, repentance, thanksgiving and hymns—indicates that these poems were destined for liturgical reading at a national mourning celebration. According to some commentators the book, or at least the first four songs in it, come from a single poet; to these chapter 5 was added later as a prayer, in order to adapt the whole for liturgical use.

Why did the poet choose the acrostic form in which to write these poems? First, it was one way of writing Hebrew poetry at that time, a way that lasted into the Middle Ages, as we can see from the medieval Hebrew liturgy. Second, the poet wanted to express all his feelings 'from Alef to Taw' (the first and the last letter in the Hebrew alphabet), or as we would say in English, 'from A to Z'. He desired to lead his fellow-believers to a complete cleansing of conscience through an earnest confession of sins. Yet this was not all. The poet hoped to show that a complete surrender to God's judgment was possible, for there always remained a gleam of hope. He intended thereby to implant in his hearers a conviction of total trust and confidence in the goodness and compassion of God, who would never leave them and never forsake them (3:22).

It is fortunate that the poet did not try to re-write his poems, or to fuse them into one epic form. 'An aspect of grief' says Gottwald, 'is not systematically described, but comes back again and again, contributing to the passion and to the rugged power of the document' (Gottwald: *Studies in Lamentations*, p. 31). This lack of neat organization, this tumult of thought, proves that the book stands close to the events and to the emotions that it intends to impart.

These songs, especially chapters 1, 2 and 4, speak about an ideal personality, the Daughter of Zion, or Jerusalem personified.

Chapter 3 is connected with the same events, but the poet looks at them from a personal point of view. It is a typical individual lament, expressing the feelings of one individual member of the community; in fact it is personal 'par excellence', for it attains a depth of feeling that a communal lament could never express (as we often find in the Psalms). Chapter 5 differs from the previous chapters in that it is not acrostic in form, nor does it resemble a lament in its rhythm. It differs also in content. It is not so much a lament, as a prayer and a supplication for deliverance.

4. THE TIME AND PLACE OF COMPOSITION

The content of the songs suggests that they were composed in the land of Judah, perhaps in Jerusalem. In all the songs Jerusalem is mentioned in the first place, and only then the general situation in the kingdom of Judah (Lam. 2:2; 5:9, 11). There is no mention of exile or of the exiles (not even in 1:7, or 5:5). The vivid description of events gives an impression that these were seen by an eye-witness. They were recorded in order to remind his hearers of the tragedy they had lived through, and to awaken in them trust in the compassion of God. He calls Jerusalem's past glory to remembrance and offers her a hope of rehabilitation in the future.

The first song could refer to an earlier situation than the destruction of the Temple, for example it might be speaking of the first exile in 598 B.C., according to the opinion of some commentators. But other songs clearly relate to the events of 587–86 B.C., to the second conquest of Jerusalem. Chapter 3 shows fewer concrete features but is consistent in its theological and heart-searching tendencies with the previous songs. It does not need to be considered as coming from a later period. Chapter 5, however, does seem to be later than the other songs, and may even have its origin under Babylonian rule. This may be so even if verse 21 does not prove that the return was expected soon. In general, then, it seems that these poems were composed in the period between 598 and 580 B.C. in Jerusalem, from within the historical situation we find reported by Jeremiah, Ezekiel and 2 Kings.

5. AUTHORSHIP

Though tradition affirms that the author of the book of Lamentations is the prophet Jeremiah, the editors of the Masoretic text were more cautious. Professor Lange showed as long ago as the end of the 19th century (1871), in his detailed analysis of the language and form of the book of Lamentations, that Jeremiah could not have been the author of the book. There follow historical reasons that speak against the authorship of Jeremiah. The Lament of Jeremiah in 2 Chr. 35:25 concerns the death of Josiah, whereas the book of Lamentations speaks about the living King Zedekiah (about forty years later). We should also note that the prophet Jeremiah never showed such admiration for King Zedekiah as we find here: he would not have addressed the king as 'The breath of our nostrils, the Lord's anointed' (Lam. 4:20). Jeremiah saw him rather as a weak king, who could not resist his powerful nobility. There was not much flattery in his answer to the question of the anxious king: 'Is there any word from the Lord?' ... 'Yes, you shall be delivered into the hand of the king of Babylon' (Jer. 37:17). Jeremiah was not waiting eagerly for help from Egypt, thus he could not have said: 'Our eyes failed, ever watching vainly for help ... we watched for a nation which could not save us' (Lam. 4:17). Jeremiah placed his confidence in God, and was opposed to all foreign help: 'say to the king of Judah ... Pharaoh's army, which came out to help you is about to return to Egypt, to its own land. And the Chaldeans (the Babylonians) shall come back and fight against this city; they shall take it and burn it with fire' (Jer. 37:7–8). Again, you would not expect from Jeremiah, a humble servant of God, such an individual declaration as: 'I am the man who has seen affliction under the rod of his wrath' (Lam. 3:1). The author of Lamentations seems, in fact, to have been a high official or a member of the king's court, one who actually witnessed Zedekiah's escape. Jeremiah could not have been there to see it, for he was imprisoned in the 'court of the guard' until Jerusalem was captured (Jer. 38:28).

Although opinions vary, some commentators believe that all the songs of Lamentations have the same author (Weiser, Gottwald). The progressive dynamic of the songs, leading from complaint to repentance and hope, show forth an inner unity and point to such a single author. Chapter 3, especially, reveals an inner experience of suffering and faith. It was the historical crisis that finally opened the eyes of this poet, who by a supreme effort overcame his own crisis of faith, and returned to a renewed trust in God. The author does not belong to the circle of prophets and priests, as is proved by verses 2:14 and 4:13; these denounce the guilt of the priests and of the prophets. Nor does the poet justify his complaints by the authority of his office. Rather it is his personal experience that constrains him to express his grief, as well as his solidarity with his brethren. He believes that he must walk with them in this way to God, for only thus can his inner suffering be overcome.

THE DESOLATION OF ZION

'How lonely sits the city that was full of people!'

The first song of this book describes the desolation of Zion overwhelmed by her great disaster. This moving poem, written in an acrostic form (as explained above), can be divided into two main parts. In the first part (vv. 1–12) the poet speaks about Zion (Jerusalem) in the third person, with the exception of the exclamatory prayers in vv. 9c and 11c; while in the second part (12–22) Zion speaks in the first person, with the exception of v. 17, where the poet once again describes the desolation of Zion in the third person. By this means he creates a transition to the following verses. We can observe in this poem a certain psychological progress. It moves from an objective, external form to a subjective one, because the poet changes his attitude from that of a sympathetic onlooker to being the voice of Zion herself. Even throughout the first part of the narrative there breaks forth in an ejaculatory prayer a deep feeling of distress: 'O Lord, behold my affliction, for the enemy has triumphed!' (v. 9c) and then, 'Look, O Lord, and behold, for I am despised'. This prayer contains, as it were, a silent reproach to the Almighty: 'Lord, how could you permit such a terrible thing to happen?!'

This prayer prepares the way for the second part, where the Daughter of Zion speaks in the first person. She speaks as a mother, as a widow robbed of her children, dragged into captivity. This shift of attitude from an onlooker to Zion herself achieves several things. It heightens the expression of anguish and intensifies the participation of the listener (or worshipper, when the poem is used liturgically). The introduction of Zion as a speaker is a means by which the poet expresses the central tragedy of the situation. It is not only the disaster of a nation that has fallen, nor is it the distress of an individual community; it is a greater person who is in anguish, Zion, the city of God, the community of the elect, a mystical body, not identical with those alive at any one time.

Zion (or Jerusalem) personified speaks sometimes in the name of the city, and sometimes as a representative of the whole land of Judah. In Old Testament thought the frontiers between the individual and the community were not strictly marked, as in modern literature. This change from the individual to the community is founded in the psychology of what we call today 'corporate personality'. This special way of thinking helps us to understand the existence of different literary types side by side. In these places where the poet speaks mainly about Zion, he used the form of a Lament; in those places where Jerusalem speaks for herself in the form of an individual, a Lament is also used, reminding us of certain Psalms (e.g. Pss. 6; 10; 13; 22; 43; etc.). Where God is addressed in the Lament, however, as in vv. 9c, 11c, 20–22, the dirge changes into prayer.

Part I (vv. 1–11)

1 The opening stanza from a formal point of view is one of the most carefully elaborated in the whole book. This marks the importance of its theme. We encounter at the very beginning a picture of Zion as a widow mourning her beloved. In this present humiliation and desolation, the poet remembers the city's former glories and splendour. This is a common element of a Lament, as in 2 Sam. 1:25, 27: 'How are the mighty fallen. . . ' But there is a significant addition here in the element of hyperbole, in calling Jerusalem 'great among the nations. . . a princess among the cities'. This serves to heighten the contrast, and reminds us of Psalm 48:1–2, 'His holy mountain, beautiful in elevation. . . the joy of the whole earth'.

The song begins in the style of a Lament with the exclamation 'How?' (cf. 2:1, 4:1, Isa. 1:21; Jer. 48:17). The city, which was once densely populated, is now solitary and forsaken, like a mother robbed of her children. This reminds us of the beautiful verses from the book of Jeremiah, where Israel is compared to Rachel weeping for her children, who refuses to be comforted, so great is her sorrow! (Jer. 31:15). After the first picture comes the second: once great among the nations, she is now a widow, helpless and forsaken. Widows and orphans were the most pitied, and often most wronged in human society (cf. Lam. 5:3; Isa. 49:21; 51:18). The third picture presents Jerusalem, once a powerful capital in an independent kingdom, 'a princess among the cities', now as a mere vassal, a tributary to another country (1 Kgs. 20:14–15).

2 The theme of the widow is developed further; heartbroken, she weeps in the night under the burden of her sufferings. There is no one to comfort her, those who loved her in the time of her prosperity have deserted her, some have even betrayed her (cf. Jer. 16:5; Job. 2:11). The thought of loneliness without comfort recurs as a leading motif in this chapter (cf. vv. 9, 16, 17, 21). The poet comes slowly to the conviction that there is no human comfort possible. The infidelity of her friends shows that human promises are unreliable. Some join the enemy, possibly from fear of a super-power, but some also for cheap gain. We learn from 2 Kgs. 24:2 that about the year 601 B.C. the Babylonian armies were joined by bands of Syrians, Moabites and Ammonites in a punitive action against Israel. Much the same situation may have occurred in 598 B.C.

3 Judah is facing her final collapse. In her precarious situation, though 'She dwells now among the nations', she does not enjoy her promised rest (cf. Deut. 12:9). Throughout the previous century Judah had been under continual pressure from Assyria, Egypt and Babylon, till her final conquest (v. 3c). Deportation is but the end of a long history of misery and oppression.

4 The Desolation is so great that it seems that even 'the roads to Zion mourn'. These roads, which were once full of pilgrims going up thrice in the year for festivals, are now deserted. Thus, the cultic festivities are paralysed for lack of worshippers, the place does not resound with their joy. No wonder the priests are sighing. The maidens grieve, because they miss those joyful celebrations, in which they so often took an active part, dancing and singing (cf. Jud. 21:19 ff; Ps. 68:25; Jer. 31:13). Zion, unable to help her children in distress, suffers bitterly.

5 She acknowledges the justice of the Lord, in that he makes her suffer 'for the multitude of her transgressions'. Therefore it is that the enemy prospers and her children are led into captivity. Her bitter anguish is not only a psychological reaction to a tragic situation, it is also a crisis of faith. 'How could God permit this to happen?' was the burning question on her lips. How could barbarous heathen invade the holy city? But the answer is not rebellion, it is only confession of sin, 'for the multitude of her transgressions', acknowledges the poet. These religious considerations burst the form of the Lament when the poet rejects the heathen thought that the gods of the enemy are stronger than Yahweh. 'Disaster has been sent by our own true God in his terrible judgment. He has permitted this to happen as a just punishment for our sins, because we did not pay attention to the warnings of the prophets'.

6 In this religious crisis, Zion is bereft also of her social and political leadership. Her princes, the splendour and the majesty of the kingdom of Judah, have fled like harts before the enemy. The enemy is often compared to a hunter, as in Lam. 3:52, and Jer. 16:16.

7 Jerusalem in her distress remembers her past. It is true that her memories make the present look more painful, but on the other hand they are also a comfort. Her memories lift up her personal dignity, and give her back her faith and hope in the Almighty. In the end, she is sure, God will have mercy on his beloved city and will restore her glorious days. She remembers the wonderful acts of God in the past, of his deliverance for her enemies; and so she takes hope for the future, for there is nothing impossible for God (Ps. 143:5; Hab. 3).

8 Yet, there is something more serious that grieved the heart of Zion, not the mockery of the enemy, but her own transgression against God. She would cry like David in his distress: 'Against thee, thee only, have I sinned, and done that which is evil in thy sight' (Ps. 51:4). What was mentioned in passing in v. 5 is here developed, and becomes the main theme: 'Jerusalem sinned grievously'. The rest is only a consequence of sin. Her sin is publicly exposed. Those who respected her in the past, now despise her. What could she do but sigh and turn her face away.

9 The reproach becomes intensified. 'Her uncleanness was in her skirts' (cf. Lev. 15:25). It was the spiritual uncleanness of sin that had brought this disaster upon her, she had not taken the warnings of the prophets seriously, 'she took no thought of her doom'. In order to obtain deliverance Zion must drink her bitter cup to its very dregs (Isa. 51:17). Possibly the intention of the poet here is to remind his hearers that it is not enough to live basking in the glory of the past, they must watch their present life and look where it leads (cf. Isa. 47:7). Zion gave no thought to her end and 'her fall was beyond belief' (NEB). There was no one to comfort her; and yet she remembered the only One who could truly comfort her and deliver her from the 'miry pit': the Lord who had once betrothed her 'in righteousness and justice' (Hos. 2:20). In her distress therefore she calls upon the Lord, and her prayer bursts through the form of the narrative: 'O Lord, behold my affliction, for the enemy has triumphed'.

86

10 Zion contemplates in horror the defilement of the sanctuary. The enemy has invaded and desecrated the Temple. 'How could God permit such sacrilege and blasphemy?' For the heathen were forbidden under punishment of death to enter the sanctuary (Deut. 23:3–4; Neh. 13:1). Is it not that the glory of God has left the Temple and the city because of her iniquities? (cf. Ezek 9:3–8). God does not live in the Temple, and he leaves it when people do not worship him with their hearts and with their lives (1 Sam. 4:5–11). Such crisis of faith bursts out throughout the Old Testament religion and on into the New Testament. The believer finally comes to understand that faith in the true God does not necessarily give earthly prosperity (cf. Ps. 1), for it can also mean sufferings and trials for the name of God and his glory.

The enemy has invaded the Temple, but has not destroyed it; that happened only in 587 B.C. Such an event would be too great to go unnoticed; consequently some commentators think that this poem refers rather to the first exile in 598 B.C. (cf. 2 Kgs. 24:10–13).

11 Then people could still exchange their precious things for bread. In 587 B.C. the conditions were totally different. Then only the poorest of the country were allowed to remain on the land (2 Kgs. 25:12). The Daughter of Zion never forgets that she represents the elect people of God; therefore in her humiliation she suffers deeply. She appeals to the mercy of God: 'Look, O Lord, and behold, for I am despised' (v. 11c).

Part II (vv. 12–22)

12 This prayer serves as an introduction to the individual Lament of Zion, where she speaks in the first person. It begins with an imprecation: 'Is it nothing to you, all you who pass by?' The exact translation of the Hebrew (Masoretic) text however sounds somewhat different: 'May it not happen to you, you who pass by', employing a well known idiom in the Hebrew language. The NEB translates it: 'Is it of no concern to you who pass by?' This verse expresses the deep shock of the Daughter of Zion at the indifference of the world. For Zion it was the shaking of the foundation of her spiritual and physical existence; therefore she cries in distress: 'Look and see if there is any sorrow like my sorrow' It is no other but Yahweh himself who has brought this disaster upon her in the day of his wrath. The idea of 'Dies irae', a day of wrath or of the judgment of God is widely known in the Old Testament. Amos foretells such a day two centuries earlier (Amos 5:18). In the book of Lamentations it is mentioned several times (Lam. 2:1, 21, 22). The poet sees this Day of Judgment in the siege of Jerusalem, and finally in the fall of the city and in the destruction of the Temple, as the decisive outpouring of God's wrath. The story of human despair is old and ever new.

'Is it nothing to you, all you who pass by?' could have been the cry of despair of those who, dumped into cattle trucks, passed through flowering fields and gardens to the concentration camps of Auschwitz or Buchenwald. The Jewish people remembers the holocaust of the Second World War as a special Day of God's judgment, the Day of Destruction, or in Hebrew 'Yom Hashoa' (Jakob Jocz: *Israel after Auschwitz*, p. 58). One of the great writers on the Holocaust, E. Wiesel, refuses to relieve God from his responsibility. Even believers like Rabbi Berkowitz find it difficult to explain the disaster that befell God's chosen people in view of God's goodness and omnipotence, except by faith. 'Even if no answer can be found, we would still be left with the only alternative with which Job was left, i.e. contending with God, while trusting him, of questioning while believing, inquiring in our minds, yet knowing in our hearts' (Jakob Jocz, op. cit. pp. 60–61).

13 The poet of Lamentations tries to express the feelings of his heart as he describes God's anger. It is like a fire sent from heaven, it runs through the bones of the afflicted. There is no escape from it. Verses 13–15 try to describe the sufferings inflicted on the city. Human language is too poor to express it. Therefore the poet seeks to express it in different images. First comes the fire, which illustrates God's burning anger (cf. Lam. 2:3; Ps. 18:8). The second image is taken from a hunting scene, where a hunter spreads his net to catch his prey. At Hosea 7:12 this image is used of God himself, spreading a net for his enemies; otherwise it is used to present the enemy spreading his nets for the righteous (Pss. 9:16, 25:15; 31:4; 35:7). The third image presents the desolation of the city, as a person racked with pain all the day long. These pains come from sufferings inflicted by the enemy; yet the reason for these sufferings is much deeper, it lies in the soul of the afflicted (cf. Pss. 13:2; 69:29).

14 Zion is weighed down by the burden of her transgressions, which is bound like a yoke around her neck, but what is worse, it has been bound by God's own hand. The image of the yoke displays the great seriousness of sin as well as a deep conviction of it. We see here the inner connection between sin and God's judgment, for it is God himself who has delivered Zion into the hands of the enemy.

15 Zion's confidence in her mighty men has been crushed to the ground. Perhaps God wanted to show her that it is 'Not by might, nor by power, but by my Spirit' that we can overcome the enemy (Zech. 4:6). God has rejected and removed the mighty men from within the walls of Jerusalem. This may be an allusion to the nobles exiled from the city. The Lord had called for an assembly, for a feast (Lev. 23:4), but this time we meet with a cruel and tragic paradox, for this time people do not bring sacrifices for celebration and rejoicing—they are the sacrifice themselves. The young men are crushed by the enemy, their blood being seen like grapes in a winepress (cf. Jer. 25:30; Isa. 63:3; Joel 3:13; Rev. 14:18; 19:15).

16 The Daughter of Zion weeps bitterly and mourns her dear ones. Verse 16 reminds us of the beautiful passage in Jeremiah: 'my eyes will weep bitterly and run down with tears, because the Lord's flock has been taken captive' (Jer. 13:17, cf. also Jer. 9:17 and Lam. 3:48). The children too are desolate. They were the hope of God's purpose with his chosen people for the future; now there is nobody to comfort or encourage. 'The enemy has prevailed'. And so the passage contained in vv. 12–16 is more than a mourning Lament, it is an acknowledgment of the terrible justice of God. The sorrow is too great for words, and Zion becomes silent for a while. We are reminded of the words of the prophet: 'Be silent before the Lord God!.... The Lord has prepared a sacrifice and consecrated his guests' (Zeph. 1:7).

17 The poet takes over. He comments on the situation and provides, as it were, a bridge between the first part of the direct Lament and the second (18–22). He now confirms objectively what we have already heard in the subjective cry of the Daughter of Zion. Here is not the exaggeration of a sensitive mother: the disaster is real and it is great.

18–22 In this last section Zion again voices personally her complaint. She acknowledges the righteousness of God, as Jeremiah did in his book at 12:1, but without the silent reproach of the prophet: 'Why does the way of the wicked prosper?' Zion acknowledges fully her rebellion. She confesses openly her guilt to the peoples around, and declares thereby that it is not the might of the enemy that has prevailed but the justice of God. He has merely used the enemy as the instrument of his wrath. Therefore her 'maidens and young men have gone into captivity' (18c). Zion is a witness to the justice of God to all the peoples around (Isa. 1:2; 2:2; Mic. 1:2). And yet we feel here a silent complaint that innocent children have had to suffer for the sins of their parents.

19 Zion complains because of the betrayal of her friends and because of the famine in the city. Yet, it is no accident that confession of sin and her complaint stand so near each other, because 'from the biblical point of view the knowledge of God and the confession of sin are two poles on which the complaint is built' (Weiser).

20 The Daughter of Zion now describes her inner distress and calls upon the mercy of God. She spreads before him the horror of her situation. For there is not only the cruel enemy that kills her loved ones in the streets, there is also famine and plague that take their toll inside of the beleaguered houses. 'In the street the sword bereaves; in the house it is like death'. She turns with this complaint directly to God, and so it becomes a prayer.

21 It is at this point, when a person acknowledges his or her utter helplessness, that a way to God is found. Where no human comfort is possible, there is still God to bring comfort to the afflicted. Moreover, he can also bring just retribution upon the cruel enemy who has abused his power, for this is an element in God's covenantal relationship with Israel (Isa. 49:23; Zech 1:15). Yes, God will punish the arrogant enemy, who boasts in his victory (v. 22). The author thus expresses in this prayer the view frequently found in the Old Testament, that all nations are under the judgment of God, and that his justice will not be complete if the heathen remain unpunished for the evil they have done (Joel 3:2–3).

THE WRATH OF GOD

The second song of the book of Lamentations is also written in acrostic form. It is a Lament, though it does not follow exactly the rhythm of one. This song too can be divided into two main parts. In the first part (vv. 1–10) the poet describes the events of the fall of Jerusalem, passing gradually from a general description to details. This first part can be again subdivided into two sections: (a) vv. 1–5, where the poet describes the destruction of the land and of the people in general; and section (b) vv. 6–10, where the poet speaks more about the destruction of Jerusalem and of its Temple in particular.

God himself has become the enemy. He pulls down the strongholds of Judah (v. 2) and blazes like a fire through Jacob, consuming all around. The prophets receive no message from above, they have lost communication with the eternal God. The elders mourn over the destruction of Jerusalem. Verse 10 suggests that this poem was read in a mourning assembly held for the remembrance of the destruction of the city and of the Temple.

The second part of the song is more subjective (vv. 11–22). The poet speaks in the first person; he is deeply distressed and weeps bitterly over the fall of his beloved city, and his heart is aching over the destruction of his people (v. 11). The vivid emotion and the terrible details of the disaster suggest that the poet was an eye-witness of these events. He perceives with anguish children dying in their mothers' arms.

What consolation can he bring to the Daughter of Jerusalem? In the whole wide world there is no comparison, no likeness to her disaster (cf. Lam. 1:12). Young men and maidens, her future and her pride, are slaughtered without mercy in the streets of the city (v. 21). Perhaps the disaster could have been averted, if the false prophets had not lulled the city into a false self-confidence (v. 14). The tragedy is deepened by the scorn and hatred of the enemy (v. 16; cf. 1:7c).

But more painful than the material loss and the scorn of the enemy is the spiritual suffering under the crushing conviction of sin (cf. Ps. 51:4). It was Yahweh himself, who had originally chosen the city for his dwelling place, who had now caused her disaster. He had executed his warnings announced by the prophets, and had fulfilled the terrible judgment of destruction (v. 17). And yet, in spite of all this, there is still a deep belief in the heart of the poet that God will not keep his anger for ever, in that in essence he is the God of mercy (cf. Ps. 103:9). The poet urges the Daughter of Zion to call upon the mercy of God:

'Cry aloud to the Lord!'
'Pour out your heart like water
before the presence of the Lord!' (vv. 18, 19).

And this is what she finally does in a moving plea (vv. 21–22).

Part I (vv. 1–10)

1 'How the Lord in his anger has set the daughter of Zion under a cloud!' As with the first song, so this one also begins with the rhetorical question 'How?' This question reminds us of a dirge, the same essential feeling occurring again in the next verse. Yet, this song has nothing in common with a secular dirge, for it speaks about the acts of Yahweh. Verses 1–9 have the characteristics of a song that speaks about God's salvation, yet this song is a Lament and testifies to God's judgment, and this we must accept seriously (v. 22). God has covered the Daughter of Zion with the cloud of his anger. The cloud was usually a sign of God's favour, as in Exod. 19:9, where God said to Moses: 'I am coming to you in a thick cloud'. So also in Exod. 34:5–6, where God descends in a cloud and declares: 'The Lord, the Lord, a God merciful and gracious ... abounding in steadfast love' (cf. also Pss. 97:2; 104:3; 1 Kgs. 8:10, Isa. 4:5). Here we must make two remarks: two words are used in Hebrew for 'cloud', *anan* and *ab*. The first means a light cloud and the second a heavy cloud (usually a dark cloud). God's favour appears usually in a light cloud, while the heavy cloud, *ab*, covering Zion forbodes a storm. This verbal form occurs only here in the whole Hebrew O.T. The effect of God's anger is terrible; as the poet sees it: 'He has cast down from heaven to earth the splendour of Israel'. This reminds us of the expression used by the prophet Isaiah: 'How are you fallen from heaven, O Day Star, son of Dawn!' (Isa 14:12). God had not 'remembered his footstool in the day of his anger'. 'Footstool' signifies here the Ark of God (cf. 1 Chr. 28:2); but it can also signify the Temple in general (Ps. 132:7, Aramaic version; cf. also Ezek. 43:7). The opening of the song proclaims that God's judgment is revealed not only in words but also in deeds. From the historical-religious point of view it is in accordance with the proclamation by the prophets about God's judgment (Exod. 20:5 ff.; 34:5 ff.; Amos. 4:12; 5:2; 8:9–10). In the presentation of the complaint we see the influence of the worship tradition (cf. Ps. 89:20–37, 38–45). Only, here the poet does not mention God's promises as the Psalmist does.

The destruction of the Temple signifies not only the loss of the sanctuary; it bears a deeper significance. It brings with it a crisis of faith, and threatens the ideology of salvation. In Israel's religious tradition, salvation is connected with God's presence in the Ark (cf. 1 Sam. 4:3); consequently, with the destruction of the Temple the question arises, has God forsaken his people? It was the conviction of Judah that Jerusalem was unconquerable, not only because of its position and its fortifications (cf. 2 Sam. 5:6; Ps. 46:4–5), but because Yahweh himself had chosen this city for his habitation; moreover its election was recognized even by other nations. This belief was expressed in the Songs of Zion (cd. Pss. 46, 48, 87) as well as by the prophet Isaiah, who was persuaded that God himself would take care of the defence of Jerusalem (Isa. 37:21–29). His belief was confirmed in the retreat of Sennacherib from the walls of the city in 701 B.C. The Deuteronomic reform also gave strong support to belief in the divine election of Jerusalem; and even when the policy of the reformation did not succeed completely, the inviolability of the Temple remained as the last guarantee against the threat of the enemy (Jer. 7:4). The fall of Jerusalem, viewed from this standpoint, signified not only a national catastrophe, it shattered also a whole system of religious belief (Jer. 26:1–19). This is a tradition that Amos had already tried to shake (cf. Amos 5:18 ff.; Zeph. 1:7 ff; 2:2 ff). The Day of the Lord becomes a Day of Judgment, the Day of the wrath of God (Lam. 1:12, 2:21).

2–9   The strophes 2–9 are dedicated to the development of this theme of the wrath of God. The narrative of tragic events serves not only as a painful reminder of the disaster, it is also an acknowledgment of the fact that God is the author of these tragic events. We see no rebellion as in the case of Job; here it is complete surrender and acceptance of God's judgment, even though it be with trepidation.

2–5   From the second strophe until the fifth, the poet speaks about the destruction of Judah, of the land and of its inhabitants as well. 'The Lord has destroyed without mercy all the habitations of Jacob' (v. 2). The Hebrew word *bila* means utter destruction, from the root *bala*, to swallow up. The Hebrew word used for 'habitations' *n'oth*, really means pleasant habitations (Ps. 23); but *n'oth* means also open localities in contrast to fortified cities, like Azekah and Lachish (Jer. 34:7). The kingdom and its princes are also victims of God's wrath. 'He has cut down in fierce anger all the might of Israel' (v. 3). His 'fierce anger' 'burned like a flaming fire in Jacob, consuming all around'. God has not only withdrawn his support but had actively supported the enemy. 'He has slain all the pride of our eyes' lit. 'the delight of our eyes', i.e. the sons and daughters of Zion. The fire of God's wrath did not spare the tent of the Daughter of Zion (v. 4c, cf. 3c), the Temple, where the people of Israel were accustomed to meet their God and Creator (cf. Exod. 33:7–11). God himself had become like an enemy to Israel, he had destroyed not only the city, but the nation as well (cf. Pss. 15:1; 48:2; and especially Ps. 87:1 ff). The Lord himself, who had once chosen Jerusalem for his habitation, had now destroyed its palaces, laid in ruin its strongholds, and so the place that had once resounded with joy had now become full of mourning and lamentation.

6   'He has broken down his booth like that of a garden.' In verses 6 and 7 the poet describes the destruction of the Temple. His 'booth' or tent, in Hebrew *sukka*, means a temporary dwelling, but it can also mean the tent of meeting with the Lord, which Moses had erected. Later the word was applied to the Temple (cf. Amos 9:11; Isa. 5:5). This he had destroyed like a gardener, or 'garden' as some versions put it; for the Hebrew word *gan* is here probably a contraction of the Hebrew word *ganan* which means 'gardener' (Gordon, Hartom). Thus we are presented here with a deeper meaning, that it is God himself who had destroyed the Temple, and not the invader, who was but an instrument in his hand. He had destroyed it like as a gardener destroys his tent in the vineyard, when it is of no more use to him (cf. Isa. 5:5; 1:8; Ps. 76:2). 'He has destroyed his place of meeting' and 'made Zion forget her appointed feasts and her Sabbaths' (v. 6b, NIV). We must remember that in those times there were no printed calendars; instead there were fires burning on elevated places announcing the approaching feasts. Such fires were, of course, impossible under enemy invasion (cf. 1:4). 'King and priest alike he scorned' (NEB).

Could it be credible that the God who had chosen Israel for his own people ('you shall be my own possession among all peoples', Exod. 19:5), and Jerusalem to be his footstool for ever, should now have 'repented' of his promises, as any of the gods of the nations might do? (See Amos 7:6). How could he have scorned his altar (built by Moses at Yahweh's command and specification), and disowned the sanctuary that he himself had ordained? How could it be that *Torah* (the very revelation of the Word of God) 'is no more, and her prophets obtain no vision from the Lord' (v. 9b)? That then is how Yahweh, the Lord of the Covenant, 'had become like an enemy' to his people (v. 5). 'The Lord determined to lay in ruins the wall of the daughter of Zion . . . her gates have sunk into the ground' (vv. 8–9).

The city had a strange history. Tradition had it that Melchizedek of (Jeru-)Salem, 'priest of God Most High', had blessed Abraham in a ceremony of bread and wine (Gen. 14:18–19). It was this city that David had captured, and had called 'The City of David'. But now Jerusalem was in ruins. This Abraham, moreover, was the 'father' of the People of God. God had brought them into being to become his instrument for the blessing of all mankind (Gen. 12:3; 22:18; Ps. 105:6). How could that be so now, when the youth who were to carry on the promise were fainting in the streets of the city (v. 11)?

The line of David, again, was God's choice for the good of all mankind. At 2 Sam. 7:14–16 we read how, through the lips of the court-chaplain, Nathan, God had said of David 'I will be his father and he will be my son . . . And your house (dynasty) . . . shall be made sure for ever before me'. But now the present incumbent on the throne of the dynasty of David was languishing in a Babylonian jail (v. 9). Worse still, *Torah* (the very revelation of the Word of God) 'is no more, and her prophets obtain no vision from the Lord' (v. 9b).

The awareness therefore of how God had broken faith with his people was both a physical and a spiritual trauma. Verse 12 describes the horror of parents watching their children crying out with hunger, or seeing the life of their babies slowly ebb away as they sought to suck from their mother's dried up breast. And so the terrible reality came home to the minds of all thoughtful people, even as they suffered the physical pain of thirst and starvation: the prophets who have gone before (v. 14) have not been faithful to their calling (Jer. 23:16; Mic. 3:5–7). They might have been saved from this ruin, which is as vast as the sea (v. 13) if only the prophets had had the courage to 'expose their iniquity'. And so it is that the world was now sneering at their fate (v. 15). Yet what had happened to them was just what true prophets like Amos had declared God must necessarily do to his chosen people, his chosen city, his chosen king, his chosen land, if he was to be true to himself and to his loving purpose for the world (Amos 3:2, 6, 11; 5:2, 16, 18–24; 6:8; 7:7–9; 8:1–3, 9–10; 9:1–6). It was not God who had been unfaithful to his Covenant; it has been we who have been unfaithful to him!

Yet we hear, not the pious chanting of godly people, but the clamour of the heathen enemy who had come to loot and destroy. The conclusion that the poet had come to was just too difficult a pill to swallow for ordinary, proud men and women. So they prefer to keep returning to the question: 'How could God permit all this to happen?'

Unable to face reality, then, we are told that 'the elders . . . sit on the ground in silence', for no word is adequate to express their agony and pain (cf. Job 2:13), and they threw dust on their heads and put on sackcloth (cf. 2 Sam. 1:2; Ezek. 27:30). As the Targum put it, it was no longer a time for social intercourse, now that the king had gone. But of course his going meant more than loss of their monarch: God himself had deserted them. The elders were the learned amongst Israel, so they could see more clearly than others the significance of events. God's promises to Israel had been concerned with the whole of her life and destiny. He had promised her her land 'for ever', as a sign that he would be their God 'for ever'. But now, this Promised Land had been overrun by the Babylonians. Again, God had clearly broken his promise to Abraham, for his descendants were at that moment scattered to the winds. It was the intelligentsia alone who could understand and interpret God's *Torah*, but they have been taken into exile: priests, politicians, artisans, teachers, merchants, lawyers, even the prophets. God's choice of Zion was now a heap of ruins, although it was that place of which God had promised 'My Name shall be there'. No longer did the ruined Temple contain the Ark of the Lord, in which had reposed for centuries 'the two tables of stone which Moses put there at Horeb, where the Lord made a covenant with the people of Israel; (1 Kgs. 8:9). Accordingly the following two inferences could be drawn: (1) God had in fact broken his own covenant, and (2) the Ten Commandments were now null and void. No wonder a fear of possible anarchy now loomed in our poet's heart (Prov. 29:18; and cf. Isa. 3:1–8).

Part II (vv. 11–22)

11 The narrative has now ended, and the poet strikes a more personal note. The lament becomes personal, for the poet is personally involved in the disaster; the events were now bone of his bones, and flesh of his flesh. He is deeply moved by the agony of the little ones in their mothers' arms. The verse thus reads like a silent reproach to the Almighty: 'No matter how justified your dealings with Jerusalem may be, what have these little ones done to suffer so much?'

13   Who can measure the extent of the disaster? The poet can find no comparison in history for such a calamity, nothing like it that might comfort the Daughter of Zion. 'For vast as the sea is your ruin; who can restore you?'. Thus our poet is beginning to glimpse that the ruin of God's chosen city is somehow unique in the world's history, in an era when few cities escaped destruction by an enemy; in other words, as we would say today, the fall of Jerusalem had unique eschatological significance.

14   The poet tries to excuse the sin of Jerusalem, and thereby give some comfort to the Daughter of Zion; it is her prophets that have led her astray: 'Your prophets have seen . . . false and deceptive visions'. Jonah was an exception; he had called Nineveh to repentance and saved her from disaster (Jonah 3:4–9). The poet implies that Israel's destruction was not inevitable; had she repented, she might have enjoyed good fortune (cf. Deut 30:3).

15   Even strangers and passers-by were moved by the tragedy of Jerusalem. They asked in disbelief: 'Is this the city that was called the perfection of beauty, the joy of all the earth?' (cf. Pss. 48:2; 50:2). The attitude of the enemy was even more painful (v. 16). At last they were seeing their dream realised (v. 16c). But these enemies forgot that they were but instruments in the hands of a mighty God.

17   'The Lord has done what he purposed, has carried out his threat; as he ordained long ago' (v. 17). The full truth of God's word was now confirmed in the language of deeds, a reality that no one could miss (cf. Lam. 2:8; Exod. 20:5; Deut. 28:15).

18–20   In the presence of the stark reality of God's judgment, there is no other way open before the poet but to address his lament directly to God. 'Cry aloud to the Lord!', lit. 'Their heart cried unto the Lord!' Some modern versions (RSV, NEB) translate the words, for grammatical reasons, in the second person singular to fit with the rest of the strophe; but there is no need to do so. The poet has already compared the greatness of the disaster with the vastness of the sea (2:13), now he compares the tears of the Daughter of Zion to an unending stream. What has happened is not a private matter, individuals dare not dry their tears and opt out of the terrible catastrophe. No, this is a national and a theologically justifiable judgment; that is why it is our duty to continue in prayer and supplication for the mercy of God. 'Give yourself no rest, your eyes no respite'. For Israel was precious to God as the apple of his eye (Deut 32:10, cf. also Zech. 2:8). Israel is now on the verge of the ultimate horror. Her sufferings could lead her now into the situation where she might lose all contact with the living God.

But the heavens are silent: 'In the dust of the streets lie the young and the old . . . in the day of thy anger *thou* hast slain them, slaughtering without mercy'. What then is the next verse actually describing (v. 22)? Through Moses of old, as our poet recalled, God had ordained certain sacrifices at which all Israel was summoned to be present. These sacrifices, when animals went up in smoke to the Lord, were made *on behalf of* the worshippers, to expiate their sin and restore them to fellowship with God. But now the Daughter of Zion was herself to be the sacrifice! She herself had become the *olah*, the 'whole-offering', not even just a part offering when only portions of the sacrificial animal went up to the Lord—for 'none escaped or survived'. And so Israel is now meeting with that ultimate horror, known absolutely to Jesus on the Cross (when he quoted Ps. 22:1), of being abandoned by God himself. This horror is echoed again for us in the closing words of the *Te Deum Laudamus*—'Let me never be confounded'. Yet God had now 'done what he purposed . . . as he ordained long ago' (as the period of Amos' life must have seemed to the poet's generation). God had now in fact 'demolished without pity' (v. 17).

What then can be said about this extraordinary sacrifice?

(a) As Hosea had declared at Hos. 11:1, Israel was God's beloved child, whom he had reared and brought up, teaching him to walk, even cuddling him in his arms. Our Lam. 2:22c adds to that attractive picture the words, 'those whom I dandled and reared'.

(b) Hos. 11:2 had declared, 'The more I called them, the more they went from me; they kept sacrificing to the Baals'. Consequently, now that the judgment had fallen, what we learn at Lam. 2:21–22 is that God had invited his child 'as to the day of an appointed feast'. Thereupon it was God himself who, unlike Abraham so long before, had then proceeded to sacrifice his own child. 'The Lord has done what he purposed' (2:17).

(c) God had planned this sacrifice, then, though it was Nebuchadnezzar who had carried it out.

(d) In declaring as much, our poet had thus laid his finger upon that ultimate reality which is true for all times and which we have seen exemplified in our generation in the Holocaust of Auschwitz. For then, to use instead the language of Acts 2:23, God's own child, his chosen people, 'delivered up according to the definite plan and foreknowledge of God, *you* crucified and killed by the hands of lawless men'. We can see this New Testament exposition exemplified clearly in Hitler and his Nazis.

(e) Was this suffering of Israel, this immolation of a whole people by God himself in fact vicarious suffering? Had it all happened for the sake of the world? It is interesting that the Qumran community, just before the coming of Christ, seemed to believe that it itself, as a small group of consecrated saints, was the heritor of those who suffered in the Fall of Jerusalem in 587 B.C.

(f) But at this point in history, viz. 587 B.C., our poet has no theological interpretation to give to the events he is living through. They just stand as historical fact for later generations to seek to understand in the light of God's later intervention in the history of his people in the Cross of Christ.

THE DAWN OF HOPE

Chapter 3 or the third song in the book of Lamentations is outstanding both in form and content. This song is also written in acrostic form. Yet, it is superior in its artistry; for not only does the first line of each and every stanza begin with a successive letter of the Hebrew alphabet, every one of the three verses composing each stanza begins with the same letter. The acrostic form of the song shows its connection with the previous songs, and points to some extent to their origin at the hand of the same author.

The song can be divided into three parts. The first part could be entitled: 'I am the man' (vv. 1–24), where the poet speaks out of his own experience; the second part contains admonishment and encouragement (vv. 25–51), bearing the features of a community Lament; moreover it frequently employs the first person plural 'we'. The third part could be entitled 'Out of the depths' (vv. 52–66). It is an individual Lament like the first part, the author being the subject. It speaks about the wonderful deliverance of God, who hears the cry of the oppressed. It can also be called, therefore, a song of thanksgiving.

Part I can be divided into two subsections. In the first (vv. 1–19) the poet complains bitterly of his afflictions; in the second section (vv. 20–24) the author acknowledges his sin, yet hopes in the mercies of God, which are 'new every morning'. Part II contains three subsections. In the first one (vv. 25–39) the poet brings in the kind of teaching and admonition that is to be found in the Wisdom literature; the second section (vv. 40–47) describes the sin of Judah and its sufferings and calls for God's forgiveness. The third section contains a community Lament over the destruction of the city. Part III again contains two subsections. In the first, (vv. 52–58), the poet calls upon the mercy of God from the depths of the pit, and for God's deliverance. In the second section (vv. 59–66) the poet continues his prayer in the name of the community and concludes with an imprecation against the enemy.

Some commentators see in two parts of this song, the first and the third, two different elegies. These could have served the author as material for his song. They presume that the author took Jeremiah for his prototype, as an example of a faithful servant of God who suffered for the proclamation of God's word. The commentators find many similarities between the songs of Lamentations and the book of Jeremiah. The poet complains that he was made to dwell in darkness (v. 6), that he was thrown into a pit (v. 53). So also Jeremiah was let down into the empty cistern of Malkiah, where there was no water, only mud, into which the unfortunate prophet sank at the risk of his life (Jer. 38:6). The poet complains that he had become a 'laughingstock of all peoples'. In like manner Jeremiah complains: 'They said, "Come, let us make plots against Jeremiah . . . let us smite him with the tongue"' (Jer. 18:18); 'I have become a laughingstock all the day' (Jer. 20:7). Again the prayer of the poet for the downfall of his enemies can find its parallel in Jer. 18:23: 'Forgive not their iniquity . . . Let them be overthrown before thee . . . in the time of thine anger'.

Because of these different themes and literary types (*Gattungen*), some commentators presuppose the existence of a dialogue or conversation in worship, at the remembrance of the destruction of the Temple. We can observe an interdependence of various sections through the unity of the basic purpose that connects them. The divergence of forms and literary types is kept together by one unifying feature, that of the care for souls. This is expressed in various motifs of comfort. At the climax of this clearly discernible tendency is an awareness of a great need for faith. And through it all, the story of the individual's experience and deliverance is clearly evident.

Part I (vv. 1–24)

Verses 1–3 serve as an introduction to chapter 3. 'I am the man who has seen affliction'. Here we see a man who rises as a witness to God's mercy before a mourning congregation. His testimony is an answer to the Lament of the Daughter of Zion in the previous chapter (2:20–22). He confesses that he himself, in his dire distress, saw in God his enemy. Yet, it would be difficult to call this part of the poem 'an individual lament' as it lacks the characteristic features of a Lament, i.e. invocation and prayer. Although the poet keeps the form of a Lament, the song goes beyond the usual purpose of one and reaches out to the mercy of God. It would be difficult to understand this song without its relation to chapter 2. The speaker justifies his witness by his own sufferings under the wrath of God. He himself has seen 'affliction under the rod of his wrath'. The expression looks, perhaps, strange in English, but it is a Hebrew idiom, *Sheveth evratho* (cf. Prov. 22:8; Isa. 10:5). The thought of the poet probably takes its origin from the promise given to David: 'When he (David) commits iniquity, I will chasten him with the rod of men . . . but I will not take my steadfast love from him' (2 Sam. 7:14–15). The poet bows finally under the rod of God's wrath, but remembers also God's promise, that his steadfast love will never desert him.

2 'He has . . . brought me into darkness'. Darkness is often figurative for imprisonment, while light stands for freedom and for that which is good (cf. Isa. 42:6–7, 16; 58:10; Pss. 43:3; 107:10–16). Darkness is also associated with God's judgment, with the Day of the Lord, while light points to hope and salvation (cf. Amos 5:18–20). The poet thinks in his distress that he is especially chosen to be a victim of God's wrath, 'surely against me he turns his hand' (v. 3). Thus he expresses the deep anguish of the believer, supposing that the wrath of God is concentrated upon him alone (cf. Lam. 2:3). And when God turns his hand against him it suggests calamity (cf. Job 19:21; 1 Sam. 5:6; Pss. 32:4; 38:2).

4–18 For lack of words, the poet describes his sufferings in various pictures, such as we find in the Psalms and the book of Job. 'He has made my flesh . . . waste away' (v. 4). The writer is crushed in body and spirit; 'he has besieged me and enveloped me with bitterness and tribulation' (v. 5). The poet often uses pictures and forms of expression coined by the tradition (cf. Ps. 32:3–4; Isa. 32:3–4). Yet, we should see not just a meaningless repetition of idioms, for the intention of the poet is to present the seriousness of God's wrath, and to use the experience of his personal distress as an example to his contemporaries. For the author in telling his story has the congregation in mind, and in this way he tries to bring comfort to the mourning assembly. Thus, at one time he presents his sufferings as an illness, where his strength is wasted away; at another time he compares himself to a besieged city surrounded by the spiritual enemies of bitterness and affliction (cf. Ps. 88:17).

6 'He has made me dwell in darkness' (cf. v. 3), but here the poet thinks about the darkness of a grave or of the deep Pit of Sheol (cf. Ps. 88:6), as we see from the second part of the verse, 'like the dead of long ago'. Here the poet follows the line of thought prevailing in the Psalms, that the dead are cut off from communion with God (cf. Pss. 31:12; 115:17). Yet we can also perceive a thought that also occurs in some Psalms and some late books in the Old Testament, that there is a reward that awaits the righteous after death (Isa.

26:19; Dan. 12:2), while the wicked will be punished and shut up in Sheol forever (cf. Ps. 49:14). The picture of prison is carried on into the next verse: 'He has walled me about so that I cannot escape'. The author is under conviction of sin, he feels himself under pressure of God's wrath from which he cannot escape (cf. Ps. 88:8c). He is bowed down under the burden of sin, which weighs on him like a heavy chain. This picture reminds us of the experiences of the prophet Jeremiah as well as of Job (cf. Jer. 20:1–3; 37:21; 38:6–13; Job 13:27; 33:11). In this prison he is not only cut off from men, but also from God, which is much more serious, for his prayers are even shut out (v. 8). The author feels that his sins have now actually separated him from God (cf. Isa. 59:2; Hab. 1:2; Job 19:7; 30:20).

9 'He has blocked my ways with hewn stones', (v. 9). The author is not only fenced in and chained, his ways are also blocked. Though philologically this verse is connected with v. 7 by the Hebrew verb *gadar,* the emphasis is different. He is not only imprisoned, but his ways are blocked with hewn stones, (in Hebrew *gazith*). This expression is not accidental, for 'hewn stones' in the Old Testament stand for a symbol of luxury and arrogance, such as the rebellion of sinful men that separates them from God (cf. Isa. 9:10; Amos 5:11). The author looks for a way to God, but he finds his paths twisted (cf. Jer 3:21); yet, he actually accuses God for making his paths crooked (v. 9b)! We have another instance in the Old Testament where God blocked the way, this time to evil, though not with hewn stones, but with his angel. This happened to Balaam, when he went on a mission to curse Israel (Num 22:25).

10 There is no doubt that the poet is terrified and bewildered by the severe judgment of God, which seems to him not only like a passive wall or a prison, but an aggressive animal 'like a bear lying in wait' for his prey, or like 'a lion in hiding' ready to tear him to pieces (v. 10). Hosea uses a similar metaphor: 'So I will be to them like a lion . . . like a bear robbed of her cubs' (Hos. 13:7–8; Amos 5:19). The poet continues the same thought in the next verse when he says: 'he led me off my way and tore me to pieces' (v. 11). The Septuagint reads here, (probably from a different manuscript or tradition): 'He removed me out of sight'. This helps us to understand what 'desolation' meant for the poet; it meant to be out of communication with God.

12–13 'He bent his bow . . . He drove into my heart the arrows of his quiver' (lit. 'He has pierced my kidneys' NEB). This comes from a Hebrew idiom, where the kidneys were considered as the seat of conscience (cf. Jer. 11:20; 17:10; 20:12). The poet is referring to his innermost heart, to his conscience. His heart aches, as it would be if pierced by sharp arrows, his faith is shattered; he experiences a terrifying crisis of faith. He is tortured by the burning question: 'How could God thus treat his chosen people?' Only now, however, is he beginning to learn the lesson of the prophet Habakkuk to be detached in his faith from material things and cleave to God alone (Hab. 3:17-19).

14 His pain increases, when he becomes a 'laughingstock of all peoples' (lit. 'to my people'). This experience becomes for him a trial of faith, which many a saint has to endure like Jeremiah and Job (cf. Jer. 20:7; Job 16:10; 30:9). Either way, to be a laughing stock to his enemies fills the heart of the author with bitterness.

15-16 'He has filled me with bitterness, he has sated me with wormwood' (lit. he gave me to drink of wormwood). Wormwood is a bitter herb; when dipped in water, it makes the water bitter and poisonous. This verse expresses then the bitter disappointment of the believer who had seen in God the Good Shepherd leading him beside 'still waters' and 'restoring his soul' with a refreshing drink (Ps. 23). Yet, it is not only his spiritual suffering that the poet deplores, he complains also about his physical suffering, for his food is mixed with gravel (v. 16). It has been suggested that the exiles, deprived of stoves, used to bake bread in small pits dug in the earth (Gordon). Thus, small stones (gravel) could become mixed with their bread. The poet identifies himself with his people in their sufferings, accordingly he expresses his utter humiliation in v. 16b. 'He . . . made me cower in ashes'; the phrase reminds us of the expression 'to lie in dust and ashes' (cf. Pss. 7:5; 72:9; 102:9); but ashes suggests especially mourning. So Jeremiah exclaimed: 'O Daughter of my people, gird on sackcloth, and roll in ashes' (Jer. 6:26; cf. also Ezek. 27:30). The Hebrew word for 'made me cower in ashes', *hikhpishani,* is used only here in the Old Testament. Yet it is found in the Talmud and in modern Hebrew literature. The poet feels that he is forsaken by God, and therefore his 'soul is bereft of peace' (v. 17); as the Septuagint translates, 'He removed my soul from peace'. The phrase means that God's peace, his *shalom,* has forsaken the soul of the sufferer, who is now in perpetual torment (cf. Ps. 22:1). The torment is so great that the poet has 'forgotten what happiness is' (lit. 'he forgot all that is good'), meaning that he rejects all thought of good. This is the consequence of the fact that he is forsaken by God, who is the supreme good (cf. Exod. 33:19; Matt 19:17).

18 This is confirmed in the next verse, where the poet says: 'Gone is my glory, and my expectation from the Lord' (v. 18). The Hebrew word *netsakh* can also be translated 'strength', as the NEB has it: 'my strength has gone'; but it means also 'existence' or 'eternity', and so 'my very existence is gone', meaning, 'I am lost' because he has lost his hope in God (cf. NEB and also 1 Sam. 15:29; Isa. 38:11; Ps. 31:22). In this almost desperate situation the writer reaches out to the mourning congregation; for he understands that, sharing in the deep sorrow of his brethren, he will be able to help them (cf. Ezek. 3:15; Lam. 2:2–9; 20–22). The poet feels that he himself is under the wrath of God, and has lost the joy of life (cf. Ps. 88:15). Here the crisis of faith reaches its deepest point, when he admits that 'his hope in God is gone' (NEB). The poet uses for the first time in this song the name Yahweh for God (ineffable in the Hebrew tradition), which out of humility he has not mentioned until now. He does so in order to express his great distress, whereby he identifies himself with the sorrow of the mourning congregation (cf. Lam. 2:13; Weiser: Lamentations, 80).

19–24 *The Dawn of Hope.* The poet does not say that he has lost his faith in God, he has lost only hope of God's help. He feels himself separated from God, because of his wrath, which the author knows to be just because of his sins. He understands that he cannot plead anything to justify himself, he can only call on the mercy of God. He hopes against hope that God has not completely forsaken him; therefore he addresses God directly: 'Remember my affliction and my bitterness, the wormwood and the gall!' (v. 19). Here we see how the poet turns from lament to prayer, to a new hope, where light comes into his darkness. So the writer has never lost his hope completely, in spite of his statement in v. 8. He refuses to fall into the despair described at Lam. 2:20–22.

20 He remembers the loyal love of the Lord, though his soul is cast down within him. The NEB supposes that the original reading of v. 20 is: 'Remember, O remember and stoop down to me'; yet following the Hebrew tradition the verse can be divided into two parts; and while the subject of the first is God, as in v. 19, the subject of the second part is 'my soul'. So it should be: 'Remember, O remember Lord, because my soul is cast down' (Gordon), and is thus the continuation of the prayer from v. 19. A ray of light shines into the sufferer's heart, and, just as previously the poet was willing to forget all that is good, now he is willing to remember the goodness of God. Though his soul is cast down, because of conviction of sin, he remembers the steadfast love of God. 'This I call to mind and therefore I have hope' (v. 21). The poet remembers the covenant on Mount Sinai, the first revelation of God's grace: 'the Lord' a God merciful and gracious . . . abounding in steadfast love and faithfulness' (Exod. 34:6). He recalls the words of the Psalmist: 'Why are you cast down, O my soul, and why are you disquieted within me? Hope in God' (Ps. 42:5). A new courage is added to his hope; he remembers what was not completely new to him, the faithfulness of God behind his frowning countenance.

22 This verse employs two ancient words to picture God's love. These appear throughout the whole Old Testament whenever God's Covenant with his people is recalled. The word *hesed* is the noun that Hosea, for example, makes good use of when he speaks of God's unchanging, loyal, steadfast love towards his people (Hos. 2:19). This love never changes, quite simply because God never changes. The other noun comes from the root *r-h-m* from which the noun for womb also derives. It occurs in the mouth of God at that moment when he gave Israel his Covenant (Exod. 33:19). The emphasis of this word is clearly on compassion and mother-love. Both these nouns occur in our v. 22 in the plural; thus they mean 'expressions of steadfast, compassionate love—a new expression thereof for each new morning!' Following it, the phrase 'great is thy faithfulness' also refers back to God's promises, and so forms the climax to this great acknowledgment of God's unchanging love. Consequently, what our poet is reminding himself of here (v. 24) is that, just as each Israelite tribe, under the Covenant, was given a 'portion' of the Promised Land for its own, so he possessed the unchanging love of God as his 'portion'—and this was of grace alone! That was why he could hope in God despite all the terrible experiences he had gone through and which he has now listed in this chapter.

What this individual is trying to say, then, to crestfallen Israel is that, in his own small experience of God's faithfulness and steadfast love, God had not only never let him down, he had actually made use of disasters to bring forth good out of what seemed to be meaningless evil. We have therefore been able now to follow with our poet as he has advanced to be able to think theologically about the meaning of Israel's 'end'.

23   The poet therefore now reaches out to a still deeper knowledge of God for himself and for his congregation. He comes to the conviction that this steadfast love of God can never be lost, even when they have sinned, for it is his nature to forgive and to renew his mercies. Thus, just at the critical moment when the poet is in danger of losing his faith, he draws strength from the tradition of the covenant people, and from it comforts his congregation. It is not a matter merely of teaching about an age-old tradition: he discovers it as a new reality, a new revelation of God's nature. In this sense the actualised tradition of the self-revelation of God in vv. 22–23 forms the brightest point of this chapter. The mercy of God, his goodness and faithfulness, at the Exodus from Egypt and the entry into the holy land, are the greatest things that the poet could rediscover in the midst of his afflictions. Thus when he repeats the claim, 'The Lord is my portion', he is drawing strength from a particular moment in salvation history. In the days of Joshua the new land had been 'portioned' out amongst the twelve tribes. But now, in our poet's case, the 'portion' he had received was Yahweh himself! Or, as the Psalmist says: 'My flesh and my heart may fail, but God is the strength of my heart and my portion for ever' (Ps. 73:26). And this thought prevails right on into the New Testament (cf. John 15:4). In this way the poet gains new courage and new hope (v. 24b) and this he longs to impart to his congregation—'God is our only hope, in this hopeless situation'. 'If God has brought us down to this state we are in, then he is able also to bring us up again'.

Part II (vv. 25–51)

25   This waiting in hope that he speaks of is not indolence, but is rather eager expectation (cf. Ps. 40:1; Isa. 40:31); and here he generalizes from his personal expereince. The poet puts the Hebrew word *tob* (good) at the beginning of the first three verses of this passage (vv. 25–27). Yet the meaning of the word changes slightly from the adjective 'good' to the adverbial meaning 'it is right' in a truly didactic manner. Verse 26 runs: 'It is good that one should wait quietly for the salvation of the Lord', reminding us of the saying in Psalm 37:7, 'Be still before the Lord and wait patiently for him'. This idea is developed in the next verse (27): 'It is good for a man that he bear the yoke in his youth'. He is suggesting that sufferings have an educational value; strict education can even be helpful to the young (cf. Prov. 13:24; 22:15; 23:13–14; 29:15). But the word 'yoke' has a hidden connotation, for it is part of an idiom 'the yoke of heaven' or the 'yoke of the

Torah'. It means that he who learns in his youth to 'bear the yoke of heaven' will be able to bear the trials and testings of the Almighty (Hartom). This verse thus brings to a conclusion the thought expressed in v. 25: 'the Lord is good . . . to the soul that seeks him'.

29 'Let him put his mouth in the dust—there may yet be hope'. This is probably an idiom of the Wisdom literature; its meaning is that only those who prostrate themselves in deep humility before almighty God can hope for mercy, forgiveness and help from the Lord (cf. Ps. 72:9; Mic. 7:17). Some commentators omit the word 'perhaps' seeing in it a sign of weakness in the faith of the believer; but it is not a sign of weakness, it is a question of the sovereign will of God who 'will show mercy on whom I will show mercy' (Exod. 33:19). (For the use of the word 'perhaps' in this sense, see Exod 32:30; Num. 23:3, 27; Josh. 14:12; the words 'who knows' are also employed in this sense (2 Sam. 12:22; Joel 2:14; Jonah 3:9.) Thus, the poet calls the congregation to repentance in humility of spirit to wait patiently in silence—'there may yet be hope'.

30 Once again he gives us a hint at a theological interpretation of suffering. The phrase used here describes the activity of the 'Suffering Servant' to be found at Isa. 50:6. But that chapter had not yet been written in 587, and so could not have influenced our poet. However, this parallel in thinking between him and the author of Isa. 53 (the latter flourished towards the end of the exile in the 540's) is important. Both authors have been affected by the destruction of Jerusalem, and both are clearly reaching forward to a common understanding of the meaning of God's action therein. Both are declaring that a sufferer must not suffer abjectly, but must positively accept suffering as God's chosen means towards a new redemptive future.

31–33 Now comes a word of consolation. The poet speaks as a man who seriously cares for the souls and the spiritual well-being of his community. He does not do so lightly by looking away from the present tragedy. Rather he perceives a dawning of light in the midst of darkness for those who in humility return to God. In order to give a reason, it seems, for thus hoping in the mercy of God, the poet answers in this passage with three verses each beginning with 'for' (Heb. *ki*):

'For the Lord will not cast off for ever.
For, (*ki*) though he cause grief, he will have compassion . . .
For he does not willingly afflict . . . '

Therefore it is necessary to accept in humility the judgment of God; for only when we bow before him in humility are we able to receive an insight into his merciful heart (cf. Weiser: Lamentations, 84). God's dealings are based in essence on his steadfast love (cf. v. 22); therefore it is not his wrath but his mercy that has the last word. The poet does not intend to lessen the seriousness of God's judgment, but he insists that even its seriousness serves, in the last instance, as the realization of his mercy. It is in the mystery of divine reality that the poet finds the primal ground for his consolation, as expressed in verses 31–33 (cf. Ps. 103:8–9).

34–36   He does not try to explain away the tragic situation of his people, or forget the horror of the present disaster; for he is convinced in the depths of his heart that God does not approve (v. 36b) 'To crush under foot all the prisoners of the earth, to turn aside the right (lit. judgment) of a man in the presence of the Most High, to subvert a man in his cause' (that is to deprive a man of justice). Other commentators suggest that this is really a rhetorical question. For such is not the nature of God, as the whole Bible testifies (cf. Isa. 61:1; Pss. 68:6; 69:33; 107:10–16). This passage thus implies that the holy God sees the injustice that is done, yet is not indifferent to it, but shares in the sufferings of the afflicted, even 'as a father pities his children' (Ps. 103:13). To say that God will not see injustice when it is done in secret, is the attitude of the ungodly. These incur God's severe judgment (Pss. 64:5; 94:2–7; Isa. 29:15; 47:10; Jer. 12:4). Yet, since God does permit such things to happen, then they must be held within God's plan, even though we cannot understand his ways.

37–38   It is from the hand of God that good and evil come for he is the true and sovereign God, 'Who has commanded and it came to pass' (cf. Gen. 1:3; Ps. 33:9; Amos. 3:6; Isa. 45:7). He is also faithful and true, and keeps his promises: 'God is not man, that he should lie, or a son of man, that he should repent' (i.e. change his mind) (Num. 23:19). God who has chosen Zion for his habitation 'will not cast off (his people) for ever' (v. 31).

39   But he is also the just God, and if he tries his people so severely, there must be a reason for it. 'Why should a living man complain . . .?' (v. 39). The second part of the verse contains the answer to the question in the first part. It is his own sins that brought upon him these sufferings. He has disobeyed God's commandments, and has shown himself unworthy of his high calling. Hence, in this verse the author considers a man's proper response, and in doing so, he looks backwards as well as forwards. By repeating the word 'man' (Heb. *gever*) of v. 1, he rounds off the poem and points to the progression in thought: this has moved from the complaint he has made against God in v. 1—'I am the man'—to conviction of sin and surrender to God's mercy.

40–41 *Conviction of sin and repentance.* This passage marks a change of form as well as of content. There is a change from general considerations to the 'we' style, which does not however demand a change of speaker. The connection with v. 39 is very close. 'It is no use our complaining about our tragic lot', says the writer, 'let us examine our ways, and return to the Lord!' Verse 40 then marks a turning point from didactic reflection to self-consciousness. This is really a conclusion reached from the previous passage. The poet shares with his congregation in conviction of sin; he is sure that if we will but examine our lives, we shall see how sinful we are. The only way to bridge the gulf of sin that separates us from God is to repent and to return to the Lord. Some commentators see in this verse a cultic form of a call to repentance (cf. Pss. 65:2–3; 106:6; Hos. 6:1). The author, in his spiritual care for his community, leads them in prayer from conviction of sin to repentance. If so, then it is a call to return to the Lord made in line with former prophetic proclamations (cf. Jer. 3:21; 4:14; 18:7–11, and also Amos 4:6). The usual cultic form of repentance is not sufficient however; it is our hearts that have to be changed if we are to turn from sin to God; accordingly the poet calls out to the congregation: 'Let us lift up our hearts and hands to God in heaven', or as Joel put it, 'rend your hearts and not your garments!' (Joel 2:13). Some commentators go still further in their comparison with Joel, in translating: 'Lift up your hearts and not your hands' (Heb. *'nissa levaveinu we'al kapayim'*).

As we read Lamentations now, we may wonder at its harping on and on and on about sin—an unpopular word today. If so, then we have not discovered from the book that the sin it deprecates is that power which leads to disloyalty to the Covenant. This disloyalty separates from God, not just any nation of mankind, but the one chosen instrument of God's plan for the redemption of the world. Israel's sin is the sign that she does not agree with God (!) whose whole being and purpose is to pour himself out in love and compassion for the ordinary people of this world. Israel's sin is thus, because of the Covenant, in a unique and awful category, so that the 'end' of Israel that Amos foretold must also be unique in its significance (see Amos 3:1–2). The poem in this chapter 3, then, reveals to us step by step what the sin is that God's unique, chosen

Son must later on overcome by his death, his 'end', if he is to fulfil, within the Covenant, the calling of Israel. And since our poet's experience shows us that God handles the individual member of the Covenant Community in the same way as he handles his Covenant People as a whole, we learn how he must handle us as individuals if we have been bound to him in the Covenant of Baptism.

42–47 *Prayer and complaint.* The prayer that the poet puts into the mouth of the people begins with a confession of sins: 'We have transgressed and rebelled'. Yet this great poet of ours does not count on cheap grace. There is a hidden regret noticeable between the verses that show 'the people have not repented' and 'thou hast not forgiven' (v. 42). For the barrier of sin is still there. The poet wants to show his brethren that complaint and even fervent prayer will not help, until they return to the Lord with all their hearts. It is their sins that have caused God's anger (v. 43). It seems that God had wrapped himself in the cloud of his anger, 'so that no prayer can pass through' (v. 44). This prayer contains a bitter complaint (vv. 43b–47). It reminds us of chapter 2. Yet, the similarity is more external than internal; we can perceive here a certain progression over the previous chapter. As in chapter 2 the presence of God is clouded (2:1) and he strikes without mercy (cf. 2:2 ff, 21). His people become a laughing stock to their enemies (cf. 2:16). Thus while in chapter 2 we heard a cry of despair (cf. 2:21–22), here we can discern, in spite of the complaint, a note of hope (cf. v. 29 ff). God will not forsake his people for ever (v. 31). In spite of the superficial resemblance to the beginning of the chapter (cf. v. 14), we have arrived here at a different stage. We have travelled by an inner progression from distress to hope (cf. vv. 25–33). The sufferings of the people are no longer expressed in rebellious language, they are lifted up in supplication before God, in order to have them break through the cloud of his wrath in a call for compassion towards his once beloved people.

48–51 *The supplication of the poet.* The rigid form of the song is unable to express the turmoil the poet is going through. 'My eyes flow with rivers of tears' (v. 48). In this way he identifies himself with the sufferings of his people, and so can declare with Jeremiah, 'For the wound of the daughter of my people is my heart wounded' (Jer. 8:21). He is full of anguish for the daughters of the city (v. 51), therefore he continues to cry and to knock at the door of God's mercy 'until the Lord from heaven looks down and sees'. Some commentators may be right in suggesting that 'the maidens of my city' may refer to the open towns around Jerusalem (Ps. 48:12; Gordon). The poet now returns to the first person singular, reminding us of the style used in his first chapter. But the introduction of the congregation in the previous passage also brings in the collective sense of this individual prayer; the latter seems to continue as the prayer of the congregation. Yet the question still remains open. Will God answer the supplication of his people? God is sovereign and is free to show mercy to whom he likes, following his own judgment (Exod. 33:19).

Part III (vv. 52–66)

52–61 *The prayer answered.* In order to interpret to his congregation the national catastrophe the author tells them the story of his own deliverance, as a personal experience. God did actually come to him in the time of his distress, when he called on the name of the Lord (v. 55). The silent prayer of v. 50 was answered, the Lord looked down and saw. Here then we have a hymn of thanksgiving for personal salvation: 'Thou didst come near when I called . . . thou didst say, "Do not fear!"' (v. 57). Unlike the passage in vv. 1–24, the persecution of the enemy is presented more realistically. It is no more a spiritual experience, where God seems to be the enemy, but the enemy comes from outside. God's answer to prayer, his approach and deliverance is here essentially different from the hope of deliverance reached in vv. 21–24. It is evident that these verses are connected with the lament in vv. 61–66. This permits us to assume that the danger to the life of the poet is related to the general disaster of Jerusalem, when its people fell into the hands of the enemy at the risk of their own lives. This assumption explains the saying in v. 52b that the author is persecuted 'without cause', as well as the fact that the same enemy soldiers are mocking him in their songs in the next passage (vv. 62–66; cf. Weiser: Lamentations, 88).

52–54 The themes of suffering, sin and salvation are brought to bear on the poet's individual situation and so on the lot of his people, for he identifies himself with them and shares in their sufferings. The poet begins his song with a lament, and then presents his persecutions at the hand of the enemy with various pictures. He compares himself to an anxious and frightened bird, hunted by the enemy (cf. Ps. 11:1; 124:7; 140:5). Then he sees himself as a hunted animal, caught in a miry pit, where he is almost stoned to death (v. 53). Then the poet sees himself as passing through deep waters, which pass over his head and threaten to drown him; (cf. Ps. 42:7b: 'all thy waves and thy

113

billows have gone over me', and Pss. 18:4–5; 69:2 ff; 2 Sam. 22:5–6; Jonah 2:5–6).

55 From the depths of the pit, the author calls in despair to the Lord (v. 55). His words remind us of the cry of the Psalmist: 'Let not the flood sweep over me, or the deep swallow me up, or the pit close its mouth over me' (Ps. 69:15). The reference to the pit and to the infernal waters set the stage for the 'De Profundis' in a language similar to Psalm 130 (cf. also Ps. 88:14–18; Jonah 2:3 ff). The waters of Sheol and of the pit are traditional images of a desperate situation. Here the enemy is not Yahweh as in vv. 2–18 of this chapter, but the invader, foreign powers like Babylon and Edom (cf. vv. 4:21–22). The poet is convinced that God has heard his plea, and so he implores him to answer his prayer. Then the miracle happens. The fervent prayer of the poet out of the depths of his existence reached the throne of grace of the eternal God. The Lord heard his cry, drew near to him, and delivered him from the power of death (v. 57a). He said to the sufferer: 'Do not fear!' (v. 57b). Thus God saved him; and not only from physical death, but from spiritual death as well. It is the latter, perhaps, that the poet feared the most, that is to be cut off from God's presence (cf. Pss. 30:3; 31:22).

Sir Winston Churchill, after his capture by the Boers, and his escape from Pretoria, writes that, in the chilling reaction of the day after his escape, when he was faced with hunger and with the likelihood of recapture, he could find no comfort in philosophical ideas, which seemed to him only 'fair weather friends'. 'I realized' he says, 'with awful force that no exercise of my feeble wit and strength could save me from my enemies, and that without the assistance of that High Power, which interferes more often than we are prone to admit in the eternal sequence of causes and effects, I could never succeed. I prayed long and earnestly for help and guidance. My prayer, as it seems to me, was swiftly and wonderfully answered'. (The *Morning Post*, 1899–1900, cited by the Speaker's Bible, 161.)

So also, the author of Lamentations felt that the holy and merciful God had stooped down to him in his miry pit, into his dire distress, to help him. He could feel his presence and hear his gracious words: 'Do not fear!' Such is the self-revelation of God that we meet again and again in the Old Testament (cf. Gen. 15:1; 26:24; Josh. 8:1; etc.). On the other hand, the poet sees his case as a legal conflict against a powerful adversary, perhaps the Satan whom we meet with in the prologue to Job, where God acts as Judge (or rather Advocate): 'Thou hast taken up my cause, O

Lord' (v. 58). The same plea is repeated in the next verse: 'Thou hast seen the wrong done to me . . . judge thou my cause' (v. 59). The notion of God as the righteous judge is deeply rooted in the covenant tradition (cf. Ps. 50:1 ff; 76:8 ff; 96:13 ff; 97:6 f; 98:9). The author sees in judgment a deliverance according to the promises of God (cf. Ps. 119:154). Yahweh appears as both Judge and Deliverer at the same time. 'Thou hast redeemed my life' (v. 58). The Hebrew verb *ga'al* means to redeem, to buy back (a slave), to deliver (cf. Pss. 69:18; 72:14; 103:4; 119:154). This legal expression should of course be taken in a metaphorical sense; it means here deliverance from the power of the enemy. How the life of the author was saved escapes our knowledge. What the poet wants to do is to stress in this passage the important experience of faith, that God had heard his prayer and delivered him from the clutches of death.

60–61 The statement in v. 60 that God 'saw' and 'heard' the sufferings of the author under the oppression of the enemy gives hope that God will also see and hear the sufferings of the community. He will hear the taunts and see the devices of the enemy. This passage points back to vv. 34–36 of this chapter, as well as to v. 50, and serves at the same time as a reason for the prayer that follows in vv. 62–66. These verses express the wishes and the prayers of the individual and of the community now seemingly united on the basis of the personal experience of the poet. This also provides the foundation for a new hope and the faith that God is always near to those who fear him, especially when they call on him in trouble (cf. Pss. 34:18; 85:9; 91:15; 145:18 ff). 'His mercies never come to an end' (v. 22). In this way our poet reveals to the congregation a way out of their crisis of faith to a new hope, one that must be experienced corporately as the People of God.

62–66 *A prayer of trust.* We see in this passage the song of thanksgiving passing almost imperceptibly first into a lament and then into a prayer for the destruction of the enemy. This prayer is based on the Old Testament expectation of a universal judgment. The salutory factor in the Lord's treatment of vengeance is the recognition that not only Israel but all mankind must conform to the divine will (Lam. 1:21–22; cf. Gottwald: Lamentations, 108). The poet prays for judgment on the enemies of his people, that they may receive a just retribution for the evil done to them. For the danger is not yet over, the danger from a Babylonian or Edomite attack still exists (vv. 62–63). The community of the faithful suffers under the burden of their mockery 'Behold their sitting and their rising; I am the burden of their songs' (v. 63). The Hebrew verbal nouns used in v. 63 for 'their sitting and their rising', *shibhtam weqimatam*, express the idea of continuity, i.e. 'all the time', as often as they sit down and rise up, he (as well as the whole community) is the burden of their mocking song. Their mockery is a threatening sign of further danger and distress. That is why the poet prays, 'Thou wilt requite them, O Lord, according to the work of their hands', in the conviction that they have far and beyond abused the power given to them by God.

Over a century before this period Isaiah had explained to his generation that God was then employing the Assyrian armies against his people Israel (Isa. 5:6; 8:5–8) in order to further the plan he had in mind. God was seeking to educate his people to fulfil the promises he had made to Abraham (Gen. 22:18). But the Assyrians had proceeded to overstep the mark with their unnecessary and unspeakable cruelty; in consequence, said Isaiah, God's punishment would fall upon them in turn (Isa. 10:12). With this in mind our poet is convinced that the triumphant boasting of the enemy of his day will come to an end.

The special merit of this chapter lies in its internal dynamic. The thought of the poet moves in different forms and ways, in order to lead his people from sterile complaint to a new hope, from the gloom of God's wrath to the sunshine of his grace. The tenacious energy with which the poet pursues his aim helps us to understand the author's pastoral care. We learn from Jeremiah that some elements in the nation, under the pressure of their disastrous circumstances, had by now abandoned the faith of their fathers. They were now following the worship of other gods, namely, those of their victorious enemies (cf. Jer. 44:3, 5, 8). Thus, the poet feared that the faith of his people might crumble under the impact of the national disaster. He leads them therefore to a renewal of faith, and to a closer communion with God. Herein lies the historical-religious significance of this chapter.

In full understanding of the situation, the poet does not try to lessen the impression of the national calamity; rather he follows it right through to the ultimate depths of human suffering, and only then continues on to that place where there is a glimmer of hope. Yet behind the poet's care for the spiritual welfare of his community there lies his own deep struggle for faith. We are thus given to see that this man's private sufferings were not meaningless, just as ours are not. They had their place in the purposes of God. For his personal sufferings were acting as a witness to God's plan for his people as a whole, in that God used

116

them to lead Israel back to hope in him. The fact that God had heard his prayer and had saved him from certain death was evidence to him that God had not interrupted his communication with his people. Even in the midst of judgment God had kept open the way to the gate of mercy. And so, through his personal witness, our poet brings his people back to a real encounter with God.

SONG IV

THE JUDGMENT

We take a step back with this poem to a period before the hope of renewal spoken of above had been reached, and return to a description of the city as it lies under the judgment of God. This fourth poem thus reiterates that it is only through the crisis of faith which God's people have been enduring that they can discover the great reality—that it is only beyond judgment that there lie forgiveness, salvation and renewal of life. And how in consequence God must necessarily bring about the total 'end' of his recalcitrant people before he can totally recreate them, 'resurrect' them (as Ezekiel puts it some years later, Ezek. 37), in order to return them to their task of being a light to lighten the nations.

The poet writes with love and compassion about his beloved city, Jerusalem, and this love he can only have got from God. He described its tragedy in striking contrast between then and now. How could the 'gold' of its inhabitants thus lose its lustre? How could the young ones, the hope of the nation, thus lie scattered in the streets? The poet describes also the tragic lot of the king (Zedekiah). He speaks about him with admiration, and calls him 'the breath of our nostrils' and 'the Lord's anointed'. The poet sees the king as the scion of David, the original anointed of God and the bearer of God's promises. How could such a thing happen to him? Yet the poet foresees the time when the enemy, and especially Edom, will be punished, and Zion will be finally forgiven and restored.

The song in chapter 4 is once again an acrostic poem. The only difference here is that the strophes contain two double verses instead of three, as in the former chapters, and is therefore one third shorter. Its unity testifies that it comes from one author, and though it is composed in the style of a dirge, it contains also the motif of divine judgment (vv. 6, 11, 16). It also begins with the rhetorical question, with *ekha*? (How?) as did chapters 1 and 2. Yet it differs from the previous chapters by a clear recognition of sin and of a just punishment (cf. 2:20; 3:34; 39). The idea of suffering that was a source of rebellion in the former chapters becomes here a strong basis of faith, leading to conviction of sin.

119

It seems that chapter 4 follows the same route as chapters 2 and 3, from lament to hope; and yet there is a difference; for while in chapter 2 the stress is more on the political side of the disaster, on the destruction of the city and of the sanctuary, in chapter 4 the stress is more on the personal side of the disaster, on the lot of the people of Jerusalem, and especially of the children. This movement has a theological basis, in that the poet now finds in human suffering a reason for God's mercy and a hope for the end of the punishment. As in the second chapter, we can see here the influence of the prophet Ezekiel, but while in the second chapter we see his influence mainly in the language of the poet, in this chapter we see it in the request for judgment against Edom. Ezekiel has said, 'therefore, as I live, says the Lord God (to Edom), I will prepare you for blood, and blood shall pursue you; because you are guilty of blood' (Ezek 35:6; cf. also Amos 1:11; Obad. 1:12, 15; Hab. 2:8).

Part I (vv. 1–11)

1–2   The song begins like chapters 1 and 2 with a Lament in the style of a dirge. It illustrates the tragic change of destiny between 'then' and 'now'. Verse 1 speaks about the gold that has lost its lustre and the 'holy stones' (i.e. sacred gems scattered at the head of every street). The poet puts his grief into an exclamation, 'How the gold has lost its lustre!' Verse 2 goes on to explain these gems as 'The precious sons of Zion, worth their weight in fine gold' (cf. Zech. 9:16). Now they have become worthless like broken pots of clay, ready to be thrown away (v. 2b). In this manner he illustrates the tragic change of destiny from election to rejection (cf. Ps. 135:4 and Jer. 22:28). Some commentators interpret 'holy stones' as 'living stones' (cf. 1 Pet. 2:4), i.e. the sons of Zion, who were an integral part of Yahweh's spiritual building, and who are now like valueless earthen pots scattered in the streets (Knight: Lamentations, 136). In these two introductory verses, then, we are presented with the theme of the poem as a whole, viz. the greatness and the measure of the judgment of God.

3–4   The poet describes the greatness of the disaster progressively from the sufferings of little children to the king's palaces. In vv. 3–4 our attention is drawn to the fate of little children, who suffer hunger and misery, forsaken by their own distressed mothers, worse off than the cubs of animals. Parents abandon their children without care as do ostriches in the desert. The poet remembers vividly the heart-rending sight of children begging in vain for bread

(v. 4, cf. 2:11). The general distress has broken all social barriers and has not stopped even at the gate of the rich and the nobles. Those 'who feasted on dainties' are now seeking for food on the dunghills (v. 5).

6   The poet sees the cause of this great disaster in the disloyalty of his people. The style of the dirge is here abandoned with a closure that reaches far beyond the lament style into a religious statement. It follows various pronouncements in the Old Testament that the degree of the punishment corresponds to the greatness of the sin (e.g. Job. 22:4–5). 'For the chastisement of the daughter of my people has been greater than the punishment of Sodom'. So the sin of Judah was greater than that of Sodom (Gen. 19:24), whose sudden destruction was easier to bear than the slow dying of innocent children and adults in Jerusalem. This reminds us of the utterance of Ezekiel: 'As I live', says the Lord God, 'your sister Sodom and her daughters have not done as you and your daughters have done' (Ezek. 16:48). Yet the line of thought in v. 6 is different from similar passages in chapters 2 and 3. We have here no word of any struggle for faith as in the previous chapters, rather a surrender to the judgment of God in all its severity. The punishment of Sodom was even easier in that it was not executed by the hands of men, 'no hand being laid on it' (v. 6b). This reminds us of the saying of David when he had to be punished for numbering his people: 'let us fall into the hand of the Lord, for his mercy is great; but let me not fall into the hand of man' (2 Sam. 24:14). Thus the poet accepts the judgment of God in the name of his community; acknowledgment of sin is no longer under discussion, as it is in Lam. 3:40. Judgment had come in accordance with the warning of the prophets and the poet now accepts it. The comparison with the judgment of Sodom thus shows that he trusts the word of God; he understands that the chosen people had to endure a stricter discipline than the other nations, requiring a deeper acknowledgment of sin (cf. Amos 3:2; 4:11; Jer. 23:14).

7–8   *The Hunger.* Verses 7–8 remind us of v. 1. Here we find a similar contrast between 'then' and 'now'. The princes who 'were purer than snow, whiter than milk' now look 'blacker than soot'. Their stately bodies that were 'more ruddy than corals' (cf. Cant. 5:10), their form cut and polished like that of a sapphire, look 'dry as wood' with 'their skin . . . shrivelled upon their bones' (v. 8b; cf. Job. 19:20). The Hebrew word *gizra* means 'form' and has nothing to do with 'tattooing' as some commentators suggest.

9–10   The slow dying from hunger makes on the author a terrible impression; he prefers a sudden and heroic death on the battlefield (v. 9). But this is not enough, hunger drives people out of their senses and leads them to terrible deeds of cannibalism; and this horrible thing is done even by the hands of compassionate women to their own children (v. 10). Here the poet sees the worst that could happen in the physical and moral destruction of his people (v. 10b). The author intends to imply that Jerusalem has seen the worst, in that the curse of Deut. 28:53–57 has now been fulfilled (cf. 1:15; 2:20). Yet in spite of this shattering experience, of the crumbling of all human foundations, the author does not return, as he does in 2:20, to the desperate question: 'How could God permit all this to happen?' Rather he overcomes his despair with the conviction that in these terrible happenings God's judgment is being fulfilled: 'The Lord gave full vent to his wrath' (v. 11). Once again, then, God's severe judgment is acknowledged and accepted. 'His hot anger . . . kindled a fire in Zion' thereby confirming the warning of Jeremiah: 'I will kindle a fire in its gates, and it shall devour the palaces of Jerusalem' (Jer. 17:27), and the language of Amos at 1:7, 10, 12, 14. The end of the verse fits its beginning, so that the burning of Zion to 'its foundations' need not be understood literally, but seen rather as the fulfilment of God's judgment.

Part II (vv. 12–22)

12–16   *The Priests and the Prophets.* 'The kings of the earth' could not believe that Jerusalem could fall in such a terrible way. This is perhaps a slight exaggeration, yet is a way of presenting the dismay of the author himself at the unexpected reversal that has taken place. The reason for this dismay was firstly the author's personal conviction that the city was unconquerable, thanks to its situation and its fortifications (cf. 2 Sam. 5:6; Ps. 48:12–14). Yet, there was a deeper reason for his conviction, namely the belief that God would never permit it to happen. This belief was strengthened by the theology of some of the Psalms (cf. Pss. 46; 48; 87; etc.). The declaration of Isaiah when Sennacherib besieged the city (Isa. 37:22–29) gave support to this belief. Thus the conquest of Jerusalem was not only a national disaster, it was also the cause of a deep crisis of faith, the confirmation of a warning that the people had tried to resist with all their strength (cf. Jer. 26:1–19). No wonder the poet sees in this disaster God's punishment, even though he had tried to lessen the guilt of the people by the excuse that they had been misled by the prophets.

13 'This was for the sins of her prophets' says the author, thinking presumably about the false prophets; they had been more concerned to please men than to please God. The prophets and the priests had not fulfilled their vocation to be defenders of the faith in the living and eternal God; therefore they were directly or indirectly guilty of shedding the blood of the righteous in the streets of Jerusalem, by strengthening the hands of the evildoers (v. 13; Jer. 23:14).

14 No wonder they were the first to be punished by God, because their responsibility was the greatest. 'They wandered, blind, through the streets, so defiled with blood.' The subject is not clear, but from the context commentators conclude that it is the prophets and the priests who are meant and who are being punished for their iniquity. In support of this suggestion, we read that when the enemy entered the city, it was the priests and the prophets who were beaten, blinded or killed by the enemy (cf. 2:20). They were now defiled by the blood of the slain (Num. 35:33; Ps. 106:38–39).

15 'Away! Unclean!' men cried at them' as if they were lepers (Lev. 13:45). The terrible irony of the situation was that those who were supposed to watch over the cleanliness of others, and to decide about their cleansing, had to cry to others 'Keep away, unclean!' Thus they had to go into exile; people said of them, 'They shall stay with us no longer'. This verse concerning the prophets and priests seems thus to be a continuation of v. 14a.

16 God had chased them from his presence that he might 'regard them no more'. Those who took part in the execution of God's judgment show 'no honour . . . to the priests, no favour to the elders' (v. 16b). Here then we find the answer to the painful question of v. 12: 'How could this happen?' (even if not clearly expressed). 'How could the enemy enter the city of Jerusalem?' A time comes when the judgment begins with the household of God (Amos 3:2; 1 Pet. 4:17).

Part III (vv. 17–22)

17–20 *The final Destruction.* The Lament continues in the 'we' style. The poet speaks about events in which he himself had participated. He was possibly in the entourage of the king, whom he loved and admired, though he was opposed to those priests and prophets who belonged to the court. Together with others, the author had waited in vain for help from abroad: 'Our eyes failed, ever watching vainly for help'. Egypt proved once again to be 'a broken reed' (Isa. 36:6), 'worthless and empty', as in the time of Sennacherib (Isa. 30:7). There had been hope, for a short time, when the army of Pharaoh of Egypt had approached (Jer. 37:5), so that the Chaldeans felt threatened and lifted the siege of Jerusalem to face the Egyptian army. But these had been but vain expectations, for the Egyptian army withdrew and returned to their own land, while the Chaldeans came back and continued the siege of Jerusalem (Jer. 34:21–22; 37:5–10). Looking for foreign help had been not only a failure but also a sin. It indicated a lack of confidence in the sufficiency of God's help (Isa. 30:1 ff; 31:1 ff; Jer. 2:18, 36 ff). The poet acknowledges his deep disappointment and guilt, as well, in moving words: 'We still strain our eyes, looking in vain for help. We have watched . . . for a nation powerless to save us' (v. 17, NEB).

18   The siege becomes more and more oppressive and it becomes clear that the end is near. 'Men dogged our steps so that we could not walk in our streets'. A kind of curfew was now imposed on the city, so that people could not move freely. So the end was coming, as foretold by the prophets. 'The end has come' was the sentence, repeated here three times, that shows forth the inescapable judgment that Amos had foretold.

19   The king and his faithful guard have now fled out of the city. They fled through the royal garden even as the Chaldeans surrounded Jerusalem. They fled towards the Arabah, the steppes near the Dead Sea; but 'Our pursuers were swifter than the vultures in the heavens; they chased us on the mountains, they lay in wait for us in the wilderness'. The vividness of the description suggests that the author must have been among them; so also the use of the first person suggests the same. The author sees in the capture of the king the final stroke of disaster, and so the poem passes over into a dirge (cf. Jer. 52:6–9; 2 Kgs. 25:3–6; and also Jer. 39:1–5).

20   The king for the author was the symbol of the kingdom and of the nation as well. He was 'The breath of our nostrils, the Lord's anointed'. So the poet continues his lament by comparing the 'then' and 'now'. The traditional conception of the king as sacrosanct and immune against all attacks sharpens the contrast with the bitter reality (cf. 1 Sam. 24:6; 26:9). In the eyes of the nation the king was the protector of his people; it was he of whom

they said: 'under his shadow we shall live' (v. 20b). It is true that
this phrase, used more than once in the Old Testament, is
attributed primarily to God (Ps. 91:1; 36:7; etc.). When it is
transferred to kings, however, it indicates the confidence of the
people in God's choice of king as upholder of the Covenant God
had granted them. Thus the sorrow is very great when the king
himself falls into the 'pits' of the enemy (v. 20; cf. 3:53); it
represents the full measure of the disaster and of the heartbreak
that the severe judgment of God has brought upon the nation.

21–22 *Judgment upon Edom and the end of the punishment upon Zion.*
This section forms the conclusion of the Lament. The poet turns
his eyes, sore from the disaster of his people, to the enemy. His
grief is especially great in that the people of Edom were
descendants of Esau, the brother of Jacob. Yet, the so-called
brethren, instead of aiding them, had profited from the victory of
Babylon, and had taken their share of the spoil. This fact caused
much bitterness to the people of Judah; and it continued to find
expression in the literature of the period (cf. Jer. 49:7–22; Ezek.
25:12–14; 35; Obad. 9–10; Ps. 137:7). He addresses ironically the
people of Edom: 'Rejoice and be glad, O daughter of Edom'. The
irony of his words functions not as an oracle of salvation for a
foreign people, but as God's judgment upon Edom for their
disloyalty against Israel. The reason for this is pointed out in
Obad. 10: 'For the violence done to your brother Jacob, shame
shall cover you, and you shall be cut off for ever'. The conception
of the cup of wrath is common in the Bible. In Old Testament
times a man did not drink to another, but handed him over a cup
of wine, thus symbolizing his 'future portion' or destiny. So, in
metaphor, God could hand over a cup to man. It could be a cup of
happiness to come (cf. Ps. 23:5), but it could also be a cup of woe,
of the wrath of God (Pss. 60:3; 75:8; Isa. 51:17; Jer. 25:15–17;
Ezek. 23:32–34; cf. also Matt. 20:22–23; 26:39; Knight:
Lamentations, p. 138).

22 The threat to Edom is followed by a blessing to Zion. There is
no contradiction between these two verses, for within the prophetic
tradition there is the idea of the mutual interdependence of the
judgment on Jerusalem and on other nations (cf. Amos 1–2). It is
true that verse 22 is not an oracle of salvation opening the way to a
brilliant future, but it is at least a word of consolation, in that the
punishment is over and the judgment fulfilled (cf. Isa. 40:1–2).

God will not exile his people again. Although this is not yet an announcement of complete deliverance, this verse is closer to an expression of hope than almost anything else in this book. It recognizes that with the fall of the city and the exile of the majority of the population the floodtide of Yahweh's wrath has passed.

Song V

A CORPORATE PRAYER

This song is different from the songs contained in the previous chapters, though evidently it continues on the same theme. The difference lies in its form as well as in its rhythm. Firstly, the song is not acrostic. It contains nevertheless 22 verses, the number of letters in the Hebrew alphabet. It seems that this form was not adopted by accident, for we find similar compositions of 22 verses, for example in the Psalms (Pss. 33; 38; 103). Secondly, the metre of this song is different too, for while in the previous songs the metre is mostly 3 plus 2, in chapter 5 the verses have mostly the rhythm 3 plus 3, and sometimes even 4 plus 3. Finally, the chapter is a 'Community Lament'.

Community Laments were composed and used in ancient Israel in times of great national distress, when the whole nation would appeal to God for help (cf. Pss. 44; 60; 74; 79; 80; 83 and 89). This Lament is a corporate prayer spoken by the whole community, the subject of the Lament being the first personal plural 'we'. It expresses the distress of the nation and makes an appeal to God for help. Thus we can suppose that the song in chapter 5 was composed for a special celebration in remembrance of the destruction of the Temple. This takes place, even today, on the 9th day of the Hebrew month Ab (about May–June in the western calendar).

The historical background of the Lament is the desolation of Jerusalem and of the land of Judah in general, after the fall of the city in 587 B.C. The land is occupied by the enemy (vv. 2, 5, 8), Mount Zion lies in ruins (v. 18), the population is oppressed by heavy taxes and forced labour duties (vv. 4, 13). The remnant of the inhabitants of Jerusalem are deprived of their property, and suffer from hunger (v. 10). The bringing in of the harvest is at risk because of marauding bands on the roads (v. 9). Public life suffers too because of the oppression of the enemy, the elders dare not appear in public places (at the gate) and the young have forsaken their music and dancing, because of the great sorrow in their hearts. The song, then, seems to have been written in remembrance

127

of the national disaster, sometime after the destruction of the
Temple in 587 B.C. It describes the situation of the poor remnant
whom the Babylonians had left and had not taken into exile. The
remnant was now merely scratching a living amongst the ruins of
the city or on the land immediately surrounding its fallen walls.

The structure of the song is simple and transparent. It begins
with an invocation addressed to Yahweh in a short prayer, and this
develops into a lament (vv. 2–18). The acknowledgment of sin in
vv. 7 and 16 divides the song into two sections, reminding us of a
similar structure in chapter 4. This may suggest that the two songs
were written by the same author. The first section (vv. 1–7)
describes how the inheritance given by God himself fell into the
hands of the enemy, while the second section (vv. 8–18) describes
the tyrannical rule of the invader, and closes with a stronger and
more personal acknowledgment of sin. The third section (vv.
19–22) begins with a hymnal song, which replaces the invocation,
and is followed by a prayer (vv. 21–22) where the Lament achieves
its purpose.

Part I (vv. 1–18)

1   The tragic situation of the land and of the people is here meant
to move the heart of God, by bringing the need and misery of
Jerusalem before the throne of grace. The poet describes the
distress of the remnant of Judah, who feel themselves deprived of
their own possessions: 'Our inheritance has been turned over to
strangers, our homes to aliens' (v. 2). It is a complaint not only
about the loss of property, but also about the loss of that other
inheritance given to them by God, the pledge of their election
throughout the whole history of salvation. It was 'the good land
which the Lord your God gives you for an inheritance' (Deut. 4:21;
cf. also Josh. 24:28). What has befallen them was not only a
political and an economic disaster, it was also and above all else a
serious crisis of faith. For God had given the Holy Land to his
people Israel as their possession *for ever*. So the people of Israel had
now lost their privilege of election and had fallen into the disgrace
of rejection. They had lost not only their possessions, and especially
their land, but also the favour of God, their Protector and
Redeemer. They had become like orphans, fatherless (v. 3) and
their mothers like widows. Orphans and widows were recognised in
the ancient Near East to be defenceless, consequently Hebrew law
had long since made special provisions for them (Deut. 14:29;
16:11, 14; 26:12). The Psalmist calls upon the merciful God as the
'Father of the fatherless and the protector of widows' (Ps. 68:5).
Thus, the verse should not only be understood as a reference to the

slaughter and deportation of prisoners (i.e. fathers and husbands) but also and especially to the plight of the defenceless and destitute remnant.

4   They feel like strangers and aliens in their own land; they have to pay for their own water and for their own wood. It is true that throughout Palestine water was precious; Israel passing through Edom had had to pay for it (Deut. 2:6), but here they were in their own land! But it is clear that the lack of water in the burning heat of the summer, and the lack of wood in the winter increased the misery of the poor remnant.

5   In addition comes the loss of personal freedom, through persecution and forced labour. It seems that they were suffering also because of their old disobedience to the Lord in looking for alliances with foreign powers, for economic as well as for political reasons: 'We have given the hand to Egypt, and to Assyria, to get bread enough' (v. 6). This can mean that because of the famine they had had to wander to Egypt and to Assyria, which was then under Babylonian occupation. Other commentators refer this verse to the past sins of their fathers when the kingdom of Judah made treaties with one power or another (cf. Hos. 7:11; 11:5; Jer. 2:18, 36). If so, then v. 6 stands in connection with v. 7: 'Our fathers sinned'. Perhaps the author is seeking to lighten the burden of sin from his community by pointing to the guilt of their fathers, following the popular saying: 'The fathers have eaten sour grapes and the children's teeth are set on edge', even though the later prophets disagreed with this saying (Jer. 31:29; Ezek. 18:2). Other commentators think that such is only a superficial impression, and that this verse does in fact contain an acknowledgment of the collective responsibility of the nation (cf. Exod. 20:5; 2 Kgs. 23:26; Ps. 106:6; Jer. 3:25; 16:11–13; 32:18). This responsibility is confirmed in v. 16 (Hillers: Lamentations p. 104).

While the first section (vv. 1–7) deplores mainly the people's material loss, the next section (vv. 8–18) goes deeper and stresses the spiritual suffering of the nation under the yoke of the enemy; this is expressed in the loss of their national dignity and continual humiliations: 'Slaves rule over us' (v. 8). This can mean not only that the Babylonian authorities rule over them, but that they had sent their lower military and administrative ranks to be the occupying forces, and these were now oppressing the population who had no defence against them. This was recognised as the greatest humiliation of all; the idea is mentioned in the book of Proverbs as one of four unbearable things (Prov. 30:21–22; cf. also

Isa. 3:4, 12; Eccl. 10:17). Finally after this description of their spiritual distress, the poet turns again to that of their physical distress.

9 The lack of safety and security on the roads hinders the regular supply of food: 'We get our bread at the peril of our lives' (v. 9). Armed bands of robbers are marauding in the open country; while the people in the city are consumed by fever, surely encouraged by their state of starvation (v. 10).

11 The brutality and the atrocities committed by the enemy make the poet shudder. Women are ravished and princes are hung up by their hands (vv. 11–12). The reference to the execution of Judaean princes is not necessarily out of harmony with 2 Kgs. 25:12, which states that only the poorest of the land were left in the country. There is a possibility that we have here a reference to those nobles who escaped but were caught; they were finally executed before the completion of the conquest. In the city where lawlessness rules, there is also no respect for the elders (v. 12b). No wonder the latter quit the city gates, the place of public meetings (v. 14; cf. Ruth 4:1). The young men are now forced to do the work of domestics and slaves: they 'are compelled to grind at the mill' (v. 13). 'Boys stagger under loads of wood' (v. 13). The whole nation is overcome by a spirit of deep depression. 'The young men (quit) their music' (v. 14b), because the 'joy of our hearts has ceased', says the poet (v. 15; cf. Jer. 7:34; 16:9; 25:10).

16 The poet feels that the sins of the people have separated them from the grace of God, that they have fallen from the privilege of election into the disgrace of rejection, 'The crown has fallen from our head' woe to us, for we have sinned!' (v. 16; cf. 4:1; Jer. 13:18). They are no more a light to the nations as they had been elected to be (Isa. 49:6). It is no longer a case of 'our fathers' who have sinned, but a full acknowledgment of their own sin. In this acknowledgment of guilt as ground and cause of God's judgment the poet proves that he takes seriously the warning of the prophets and bows in humble repentance before the justice of God.

17–18 The complaint now becomes more pointed than a mere fruitless lament when it considers the full consequences of sin. There is now a real 'sorrow unto repentance' as the apostle Paul would say (2 Cor. 7:10): 'our heart has become sick', 'our eyes have grown dim'. For with the Temple lying in ruins all hope for reconciliation and communication with God had disappeared.

Part II (vv. 19–22)

Despite that terrible fact, however, Israel's faith, anchored in the tradition of the past, bursts forth with a victorious cry: 'But thou, O Lord, doest reign for ever; thy throne endures to all generations'. Here then is a faith that is greater than the Temple, in fact, the faith that the whole world is his footstool (cf. Isa. 66:1; Pss. 99:5; 132:7). No building can comprehend him, for the whole earth is full of his glory (Isa. 6:3; 40:21–23). Thus, though the Temple has been consumed by fire, God's kingdom remains untouched, for he is above the winds of change in historical events. This belief in the spiritual reality of the kingdom of God beyond space and time has now given the congregation new strength to lift up their hands and hearts to God. This expression of faith is anchored in a fixed liturgical form (cf. Pss. 9:7–8; 44:4–5; 47:2–9; 74:12 f; 80:1–2; 89:1–18; 102:13, 28; 145:13). The spiritual reserves of strength through faith, which were alive in the tradition, became active anew in this the most terrible crisis of faith in all Israel's history, and becomes the source of a new hope (Jer. 3:14–18). That this was possible at all is the merit of the prophets, who always protested against any connection of Yahweh with his sanctuary or other cultic institutions, as when Amos called in his prophetic voice: 'Seek me and live; but do not seek Bethel' (Amos 5:4 f; cf. also Jer. 7:1–15; Mic. 3:11). On this spiritual foundation the congregation now stands, and it also forms the ground of appeal from the wrath of God to his everlasting mercy.

20–21   The poet cannot believe that God has forsaken his people for ever. His deep faith tells him that God's essence is mercy and love and not wrath and judgment. And yet, he asks with anguish: 'Why dost thou forget us for ever, why dost thou so long forsake us?' One thing is clear, the author seeks communion with God; and he leads his congregation, through acknowledgment of their sins and humble repentance, in prayer for forgiveness and restoration: 'Restore us to thyself, O Lord, that we may be restored! Renew our days as of old!' The Targum translates it: 'Bring us back unto thee in full repentance', or in other words, 'bring us back from the ways of sin into the nearness of thy presence, in complete devotion to thee'. Such restoration can come by grace alone, to which the sinner has no right whatsoever. 'Renew our days as of old!' (v. 21b). This is a prayer for the renewal of the ancient covenant with God. The Targum is again more explicit in its translation of this verse, saying: 'Renew our days as good as of old' (cf. 2:1; Pss. 80:3, 19; 85:2, 7; 126:1). This is a prayer for renewal not only of the legal

131

covenant between God and his people, but also of the covenant of love, as between father and child (Hos. 11:1), or as between a bridegroom and his bride (Jer. 2:2; Hos. 2:16). In this light the promises of the prophets for the renewal of Israel gain a new significance.

22 Yet the worshipper is far from counting on cheap grace. He is fully aware that he depends entirely on God's mercy. Therefore his conscience is tortured by doubt: 'Or hast thou utterly rejected us? Art thou exceedingly angry with us?' (v. 22). The poet admits that there is still a possibility of rejection, if they do not return with their whole heart (cf. Hos. 6:1). We must also remember that this song was written for future generations as well (Ps. 102:18–22), and therefore contains a stern warning for all believers. The Hebrew (Rabbinic) tradition adds here a verse 23, in repetition of v. 21: 'Restore us unto thyself, O Lord, that we may be restored . . .' in order to soften the bitter impression of v. 22, and to allow the poem to close with a note of hope. So does also Jeremiah in his prophecy, saying: 'Hast thou utterly rejected Judah?' for he too closes with a similar note of hope: 'Art thou not he, O Lord our God? We set our hope on thee' (Jer. 14:19, 22). The repetition of v. 21 at the end of the chapter was probably due to Rabbinic tradition. Closing the chapter with a note of hope occurs in other instances in Scripture, as for example the addition at the end of the book of Isaiah, at 66:23, at the end of the book of Malachi, at 4:5, and at the end of Ecclesiastes, at 12:13.

Therein then lies the inner dynamic of this book. The poet leads his people step by step to make this mighty discovery, that through wrath and judgment, acknowledgement of sin and repentance, Israel may discover that 'God's steadfast love never ceases, and his mercies are new every morning—for great is his faithfulness'.

BIBLIOGRAPHY

1. COMMENTARIES

Michael Berenbaum: *The Vision of the Void, Theological reflections on the work of Elie Wiesel* (Wesleyan University Press, Middletown-Connecticut, 1979).

Corrie ten Boom: *The Hiding Place* (Washington Depot, Connecticut, 1971).

Robert Gordis: *The Song of Songs and Lamentations* (Ktav-Publ. House, New York, 1954).

Sh. L. Gordon: *Lamentations in 'Five Scrolls'* (Hebrew) (Massada Ltd., Tel-Aviv, 1953).

Norman K. Gottwald: *Studies in the Book of Lamentations* (SCM Press Ltd., London, 1954).

Donald Guthrie: *Text and Versions in the 'Lion Handbook to the Bible'* (Lion Publishing, Berkhamsted, Herts, 1973).

A. Sh. Hartom: *Lamentations in 'Five Megilloth'* (Hebrew) The Commentary on the Bible, vol. III. (J. Ornstein, 'Yabneh' Ltd., Tel-Aviv, 1972).

Matthew Henry: *Lamentations in the 'Commentary on the whole Bible'* vol. VI (Fleming H. Reyell Co., New Jersey, 1912).

A. S. Herbert: *Lamentations in 'Peake's Commentary on the Bible'* (Nelson & Sons Ltd., London–Edinburgh, 1962).

R. Delbert Hillers: *Lamentations in the 'Anchor Bible'* (Doubleday & Co., New York, 1972).

John A. Hutton: *Lamentations in the 'Speaker's Bible'* Introduction: H. Snaith. (Aberdeen, 1944).

Jakob Jocz: *Israel after Auschwitz in 'The Witness of the Jews to God'*, ed. David Torrance (The Handsel Press, 1982).

George A. F. Knight: *Esther, Song of Songs, Lamentations* (SCM Press Ltd., London, 1955).

John P. Lange: *Lamentations*, Trans. and Edit. P. Schaff. (Zondervan Publ. House, Michigan, 1871).

Norman W. Porteous: *Living the Mystery*, Collected Essays (Basil Blackwell, Oxford, 1967).

J. A. Selbie: *Lamentations* in Hastings' 'A Dictionary of the Bible', Vol. III (T. & T. Clark, Edinburgh, 1900).

Hermann L. Strack: *The Text of the Old Testament*, in Hastings' 'Dictionary of the Bible' (T. & T. Clark, Edinburgh, 1902).

Artur Weiser: *Lamentations* (German) Das Alte Testament Deutsch, 16/2 (Göttingen, Vandenhoeck & Ruprecht, 1958).

Artur Weiser: *Introduction to the Old Testament*, Trans. D. M. Barton. Publ. (Darton, Longman & Todd, London, 1961).

Elie Wiesel: *Night, Dawn, the Accident* Three Tales, Trans. S. Rodway. (Robson Books Ltd., London, 1974).

2. ORIGINAL AUTHORITY

The Babylonian Talmud: Order Baba-Bathra, Benvenesti, Amsterdam, 1740.

3. VERSIONS

AV   The Holy Bible, Authorised or King James Version (KJV).

LB   The Living Bible, Paraphrased, Tyndal House Publishers, Wheaton, 1971.

NASB New American Standard Bible, Foundation Press, Anaheim, 1975.

NEB   The New English Bible, Publ. The Bible Societies, 1972.

NIV   Holy Bible, New International Version, Hodder & Stoughton, London, 1979.

RSV   The Holy Bible, Revised Standard Version, Oxford University Press, London 1952.

SB   La Sainte Bible (The Bible of Jerusalem) Les Editions Cerf, Paris, 1956.